First World War
and Army of Occupation
War Diary
France, Belgium and Germany

41 DIVISION
124 Infantry Brigade
Durham Light Infantry
20th Battalion
1 March 1918 - 28 February 1919

WO95/2643/3

The Naval & Military Press Ltd
www.nmarchive.com
Published in association with The National Archives

Published by

The Naval & Military Press Ltd

Unit 10 Ridgewood Industrial Park,

Uckfield, East Sussex,

TN22 5QE England

Tel: +44 (0) 1825 749494

www.naval-military-press.com

www.nmarchive.com

This diary has been reprinted in facsimile from the original. Any imperfections are inevitably reproduced and the quality may fall short of modern type and cartographic standards.

© Crown Copyright
Images reproduced by permission of The National Archives, London, England, 2015.

Contents

Document type	Place/Title	Date From	Date To
Heading	WO95/2643 (3)		
Heading	41st Division 124th Infy Bde 20th Bn Durham Lt Infy 1918 Mar-1919 Feb From 123 Bde To 3 Div 3 Northern Bde		
Heading	War Diary 20th Battn. The Durham Light Infantry March 1918		
War Diary	Camposampiero	01/03/1918	02/03/1918
War Diary	In The Train	03/03/1918	06/03/1918
War Diary	Doullens And Ivergny	07/03/1918	07/03/1918
War Diary	Ivergny	08/03/1918	17/03/1918
War Diary	Warluzel	18/03/1918	21/03/1918
War Diary	In The Train	22/03/1918	22/03/1918
War Diary	Favreuil.	22/03/1918	22/03/1918
War Diary	In War of Vaulx	23/03/1918	23/03/1918
War Diary	Vaulx	24/03/1918	24/03/1918
War Diary	Favreuil.	25/03/1918	25/03/1918
War Diary	Bihucourt	25/03/1918	25/03/1918
War Diary	Gommecourt	26/03/1918	27/03/1918
War Diary	Bienvillers Au-Bois.	28/03/1918	28/03/1918
War Diary	Gommecourt	28/03/1918	29/03/1918
War Diary	Bucquoy	30/03/1918	31/03/1918
Heading	Appendices I & II.		
Operation(al) Order(s)	20th Bn. Durham Light Infantry Order No. 62	01/03/1918	01/03/1918
Operation(al) Order(s)	20th Bn. Durham Light Infantry. Order No. 64.	21/03/1918	21/03/1918
Heading	41st Division. 124th Infantry Brigade Came from 123rd Bde. 17.3.18. War Diary 20th Battalion The Durham Light Infantry April 1918		
War Diary	Bucquoy	01/04/1918	01/04/1918
War Diary	Bienvillers	02/04/1918	02/04/1918
War Diary	Halloy	03/04/1918	03/04/1918
War Diary	Bonnieres	04/04/1918	04/04/1918
War Diary	Steenvorde	05/04/1918	07/04/1918
War Diary	Steenvorde Area	08/04/1918	08/04/1918
War Diary	In The Line (Reserve)	09/04/1918	14/04/1918
War Diary	In The Line	15/04/1918	30/04/1918
Operation(al) Order(s)	20th Bn. Durham Light Infantry Order No. 65.	02/04/1918	02/04/1918
Miscellaneous	20th Bn. Durham Light Infantry Entraining Orders. App II	03/04/1918	03/04/1918
Operation(al) Order(s)	20th Bn. Durham Light Infantry Order No. 66. App III	07/04/1918	07/04/1918
Operation(al) Order(s)	20th Bn. Durham Light Infantry. Order No. 67. App IV	08/04/1918	08/04/1918
War Diary	In The Line	01/05/1918	02/05/1918
War Diary	In Camp	03/05/1918	11/05/1918
War Diary	In The Line	12/05/1918	25/05/1918
War Diary	In Camp	26/05/1918	28/05/1918
War Diary	Brake Camp	29/05/1918	02/06/1918
Operation(al) Order(s)	Appendix I 20th Bn. Durham Light Infantry Order No. 68.	11/05/1918	11/05/1918
Operation(al) Order(s)	Appendix II 20th Bn. Durham Light Infantry. Order No. 69	19/05/1918	19/05/1918

Type	Description	Start	End
Operation(al) Order(s)	Appendix III 20th Bn. Durham Light Infantry. Order No. 70.	24/05/1918	24/05/1918
War Diary	In Camp	01/06/1918	03/06/1918
War Diary	In Ballets	04/06/1918	30/06/1918
Operation(al) Order(s)	Appendix I 20th Bn. Durham Light Infantry. Order No. 71	02/06/1918	02/06/1918
Operation(al) Order(s)	Appendix II 20th Bn. Durham Light Infantry Order No. 72.	08/06/1918	08/06/1918
Operation(al) Order(s)	Appendix III 20th Bn. Durham Light Infantry Order No. 73.	24/06/1918	24/06/1918
Operation(al) Order(s)	20th Bn. Durham Light Infantry Order No. 75. App 4	29/06/1918	29/06/1918
Operation(al) Order(s)	Appendix V. 20th Bn. Durham Light Infantry Order No. 76.	30/06/1918	30/06/1918
War Diary	In Trenches	01/07/1918	05/07/1918
War Diary	Bildofs	06/07/1918	06/07/1918
War Diary	In The Trenches	07/07/1918	11/07/1918
War Diary	Billets	12/07/1918	17/07/1918
War Diary	In Trenches	18/06/1918	24/06/1918
War Diary	In Trenches	25/07/1918	31/07/1918
Operation(al) Order(s)	20th Bn. Durham Light Infantry Order No. 77 App I	04/07/1918	04/07/1918
Operation(al) Order(s)	20th Bn. Durham Light Infantry. Order No. 78 App II	09/07/1918	09/07/1918
Operation(al) Order(s)	20th Bn. Durham Light Infantry. Order No. 79 App III		
Operation(al) Order(s)	20th. Bn. Durham Light Infantry. Order No. 79	14/07/1918	14/07/1918
Operation(al) Order(s)	20th Bn & Durham Light Infantry. Order No. 80 App IV	16/07/1918	16/07/1918
Miscellaneous	1st Amendment To Order No. 80.	16/07/1918	16/07/1918
Operation(al) Order(s)	20th Bn. Durham Light Infantry Order No. 81 App V	19/07/1918	19/07/1918
Operation(al) Order(s)	20th Bn. Durham Light Infantry. Order No. 82 App VI	24/07/1918	24/07/1918
War Diary	In Trenches	01/08/1918	31/08/1918
Operation(al) Order(s)	20th Bn. Durham Light Infantry. Order No. 83 App I		
Operation(al) Order(s)	20th Bn. Durham Light Infantry. Order No. 84 App II	05/09/1918	05/09/1918
Operation(al) Order(s)	20th Bn. Durham Light Infantry. Order No. 86 App III	09/08/1918	09/08/1918
Operation(al) Order(s)	20th Bn Durham Light Infantry. Order No. 87 App IV	23/08/1918	23/08/1918
Operation(al) Order(s)	20th Bn Durham L I Order No. 89 App V	28/08/1918	28/08/1918
War Diary	In Trenches	01/09/1918	02/09/1918
War Diary	In Trenches Billets	02/09/1918	02/09/1918
War Diary	In Trenches	03/09/1918	05/09/1918
War Diary	In Trenches Billets	05/09/1918	09/09/1918
War Diary	Billets & Trenches	10/09/1918	14/09/1918
War Diary	In Bilets	15/09/1918	27/09/1918
War Diary	In Field	28/09/1918	30/09/1918
Operation(al) Order(s)	20th Bn. Durham Light Infantry Order No. 91 App I	01/09/1918	01/09/1918
Operation(al) Order(s)	20th Bn. Durham Light Infantry Order No. 94 App II		
War Diary	In Field	01/10/1918	05/10/1918
War Diary	In Bivouak	06/10/1918	07/10/1918
War Diary	In Billets	08/10/1918	12/10/1918
War Diary	Trenches	13/10/1918	16/10/1918
War Diary	Billets	17/10/1918	24/10/1918
War Diary	Trenches	25/10/1918	26/10/1918
War Diary	Billets	27/10/1918	31/10/1918
War Diary	Trenches	01/11/1918	04/11/1918
War Diary	Billets	05/11/1918	30/11/1918
Operation(al) Order(s)	20th Bn. Durham Light Infantry Order No. 99 App I	09/11/1918	09/11/1918
Operation(al) Order(s)	20th Bn. Durham Light Infantry Order No 101. App II	17/11/1918	17/11/1918
Operation(al) Order(s)	20th Bn. Durham Light Infantry Order No. 102 App III		
War Diary	Billets Bievene	01/12/1918	11/12/1918

War Diary	Billets Enghien	12/12/1918	12/12/1918
War Diary	Billets Hal	13/12/1918	13/12/1918
War Diary	Billets Waterloo	14/12/1918	15/12/1918
War Diary	Billets Genappe	16/12/1918	16/12/1918
War Diary	Billets Ligny	17/12/1918	17/12/1918
War Diary	Billets Spy	18/12/1918	18/12/1918
War Diary	Billets Champion	19/12/1918	19/12/1918
War Diary	Billets Antheit	20/12/1918	31/12/1918
Operation(al) Order(s)	20th Bn. Durham Light Infantry Order No. 103 App I	11/12/1918	11/12/1918
Operation(al) Order(s)	20th Bn. Durham Light Infantry Order No. 104 App II	12/12/1918	12/12/1918
Operation(al) Order(s)	20th Bn. Durham Light Infantry Order No. 105 App III	13/12/1918	13/12/1918
Operation(al) Order(s)	20th Bn. Durham Light Infantry Order No. 106 App IV	15/12/1918	15/12/1918
Operation(al) Order(s)	20th Bn. Durham Light Infantry Order No. 107 App V	16/12/1918	16/12/1918
Operation(al) Order(s)	20th Bn. Durham Light Infantry Order No. 108 App VI	17/12/1918	17/12/1918
Heading	London Division (Late 41st Division) 124th Infy Bde 20th Bn Durham Lt Infy Jan-Feb 1919		
War Diary	Billets Antheit	01/01/1919	06/01/1919
War Diary	Billets Engels Kirchen	07/01/1919	12/01/1919
War Diary	Outposts Engels Kirchen	13/01/1919	31/01/1919
Operation(al) Order(s)	20th Bn. Durham Light Infantry Order No. 111 App I	05/01/1919	05/01/1919
Miscellaneous			
Miscellaneous	List Of Pamphlets & Books		
Miscellaneous			
Miscellaneous	List Of Files		
War Diary	Outposts Engelskirchen	01/02/1919	10/02/1919
War Diary	Ehreshoven	11/02/1919	15/02/1919
War Diary	Billets Ehreshoven	16/02/1919	27/02/1919
War Diary	Baaracks Riehl	28/02/1919	28/02/1919

WD 95/2643(3)

WD 97/2643(3)

41ST DIVISION
124TH INFY BDE

20TH BN DURHAM LT INFY

~~MAR - DEC 1918~~

1918 MAR — 1919 FEB

~~To 3 DIV~~

FROM 123 BDE

To 3 DIV ~~~~

3 NORTHERN BDE

124th Inf.Bde.
41st Div.

Battn. transferred
from 123rd Inf.Bde.
41st Div. 17.3.18.

Battn. returned to
France from Italy
2/9.3.18.

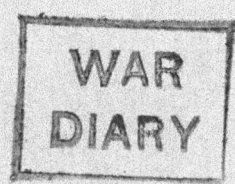

20th BATTN. THE DURHAM LIGHT INFANTRY.

M A R C H

1 9 1 8

Attached:-

Appendices I & II.

WAR DIARY
of the 21st S. Bath. Durham L.I.
INTELLIGENCE SUMMARY.

Army Form C. 2118.

Place	Date	Hour	Summary of Events and Information	Remarks and references to Appendices
CAMPOSAM-PIERO.	1/3/18		Companies were at the disposal of Company Commanders for training during the day. JRP	
DITTO	2/3/18		During the morning the Commanding Officer inspected all Companies in full marching order on their various parade grounds. In the afternoon Companies carried out Recreational training. JRP	
	3/3/18	4.30 pm	Half Headquarters Coy & half the Transport entrained from CAMPOSAMPIERE. Station at 4.30 pm. JRP	App I
		8.30 AM	The right half Batt. with remainder of Headquarters Coy & Transport entrained from same place at 8.30 A.M. JRP	
In the train	4/3/18 5/3/18 6/3/18		In the train. JRP	
DOULLENS AND IVERGNY	7/3/18		The left half Batt. etc. arrived at DOULLENS where they detrained & marched to billets at IVERGNY which they reached about 11.30 A.M. The remainder of the day was devoted to Recreational training. JRP	

WAR DIARY
INTELLIGENCE SUMMARY

of the 2nd S. Batt. D.L.I.

Army Form C. 2118.

(Erase heading not required.)

Place	Date	Hour	Summary of Events and Information	Remarks and references to Appendices
IVERGNY	8/3/18		The day was devoted to a general cleaning up of equipments & smartening up in the appearance of the men which was badly needed after the train journey. The remainder of the Batt arrived in the early hours of the morning with rifles & rested until midday. In the afternoon they cleaned up their equipments &c.	
IVERGNY	9/3/18		The left half Batt. paraded under Coy. arrangements for steady drill & arms drill & Physical training during the morning & they devoted the afternoon to Recreational training. G.R.P.J. Being Sunday the Batt. paraded for C. of E. Service at 11AM. Roman Catholics paraded for Service at 10.30AM & 11AM respectively. Summertime came into force at midnight 9/10th March 1918.	Uncomfortable & Summertime
IVERGNY	10/3/18			
DITTO	11/3/18		A. & B. Coys were on the range during the morning, & C. & D. Coys were a during the afternoon & the Battalion went to the baths by coys. One hour for respirator drill was carried out. A18.	

WAR DIARY
of the 20th S. Battn Durham L.I.
INTELLIGENCE SUMMARY.

Army Form C. 2118.

Place	Date 1918	Hour	Summary of Events and Information	Remarks and references to Appendices
MERGNY	April 12		The Batt. marched to the training ground in LUCHEUX FOREST & the coys. trained until 12.30 p.m. in "Equipment for attack" assault & consolidation of a position. Scouts & Signallers trained under their respective Commanders. In the afternoon the Battalion practised an attack through the wood. "A" coy acted as the enemy & practised a withdrawal. AB	
	13		"A" coy was on the range in the morning & "B" coy in the afternoon. During the morning B.C.'s 'B' had the Lewis gun drill & later hours musketry. "C" & "D" coys also had some training in the use of covering fire. "C" & "D" coys devoted the afternoon to recreational training. AB	
	14		"A" & "B" coys were on the range in the morning & "C" & "D" coys in the afternoon. In the morning "C" & "D" coys trained in musketry, steady drill, bayonet fighting, & lining up for an attack. "A" & "B" coys played football in the afternoon. Box respirators were worn for one hour by all ranks. AB	

WAR DIARY
of the 20th Battn Durham L.I.
INTELLIGENCE SUMMARY

Army Form C. 2118.

Place	Date 1918	Hour	Summary of Events and Information	Remarks and references to Appendices
IVERGNY	March 15th		The Battn had a route march which lasted for 4 hours. The Lewis gunners were on the range. The afternoon was devoted to recreational training. AB	
	16th		The Battn had 1 hour P.T. & B.F. Coy Commanders lectured their Coys on Tanks. The remainder of the morning was devoted to cleaning up. The afternoon was devoted to recreational training. AB	
	17th		The Battn was transferred to the 124 Inf Brigade. The Battn. march to the 124 Brigade area to WARLUZEL. The bands of the 10th Queens & the 26th Royal Fus played the Battn into the new brigade. 2nd Lts F.W. PALEY, A.C.W. NEW, DICK, WREN & Lt Adm. A. HIGHAM, 3rd W. Roy Fus. joined (Battn (Diol. a tactical scheme (deployment for attack ext.) For the last 2 days the Battn had in the morning.	
WARLUZEL	18th		Battn ready to move at two hours notice as instructed by Brigade. At 1.30 p.m. orders were received to the effect that the Battalion had to be a starting point by 3.55 p.m. This entailed was that the Battalion would	

WAR DIARY
of 20th S.B. Durham L.I.
INTELLIGENCE SUMMARY.
(Erase heading not required.)

Army Form C. 2118.

Place	Date Hour	Summary of Events and Information	Remarks and references to Appendices
WARLUZEL	1918 March 18th (contd)	have to march off at 2.20 p.m. The Battn was ready in fighting order with an extra 60 rounds per man & two of the next days rations served by 2.25 p.m. Just before marching off word was received that is was a practice turn out only. The Battn marched to the Brigade starting point & then formed up in a field where the received a lecture by Major EDULON on P.T. & B.F. AB.	
	19th	The Battn was inspected by the G.O.C. 124 Inf. Brigade. The G.O.C. expressed entire satisfaction in the "turn out" of the Battalion especially the transport. AB	
-do-	20th	The Battalion travel under Company arrangements Half "B" Echelon of the transport proceeded by route march to SAULTY STATION and Entrained for ALBERT. branch the HÉNENCOURT Q.G.	
-do-	21st	The Battalion arose the at 11.30 pm and marched to SAULTY STATION and entrained for ALBERT. Casualties Other Ranks wounded 1. On arrival at ALBERT the Battalion was ordered to proceed on by train to FACHET -LE-GRAND where it arrived about 2am. After detraining the Battn marched to	APP II

Army Form C. 2118.

WAR DIARY
or
INTELLIGENCE SUMMARY.
(Erase heading not required.)

Instructions regarding War Diaries and Intelligence Summaries are contained in F.S. Regs., Part II. and the Staff Manual respectively. Title pages will be prepared in manuscript.

Place	Date March	Hour	Summary of Events and Information	Remarks and references to Appendices
FAVREUIL	22nd		FAVREUIL where it occupied a camp at about 8 am. About 8 am. moved to Staind by was received and about 10.30 am. the Battalion moved up to hold the outpost line behind VAULX – VRAUCOURT. The advance was carried out in artillery formation. On arrival about 12.30 pm the Battalion bivouacked the trenches which it was holding about 5 pm the Division in front of the Battalion retired and the enemy received VAULX – VRAUCOURT. The rest of the night passed uneventfully. Very active patrolling was maintained throughout the night. Casualties OR killed 3 wounded 15 NCO's 1 OR.	
In front of VAULX.	23rd.		About 8 am the Enemy launched an attack against his two right Companies of the Battalion which was successfully resisted by rifle and machine gun fire. The attack was made by about 1000 and was met with practically no rifle. The attack was repulsed at intervals during the day but each attack was likewise repulsed. Capt. JOHNSON 2nd Lt. KAY and 2nd Lt. TOMPSON were wounded. Casualties Other Ranks killed 18 wounded during the night of 23/24th. NYDD: 52 was quiet except for active patrolling.	
VAULX	24th		Of 24th information was received that the Division on our right had fallen back. At 5 pm in consequence of this withdrawal on our	

Place	Date	Hour	Summary of Events and Information	Remarks and references to Appendices
VAULX.	1918 March 24th		night the Battalion, on receipt of orders, withdrew to a line through FAVREUIL and Augm. The withdrawal was carried out in an orderly manner and fire kept up on the Enemy. Casualties:- Officers, wounded 2Lt. A BROWN. Other Ranks: killed 2. wounded 33. missing 15. Gas.	
FAVREUIL.	25th		At 1 am. orders were received for the Battalion to withdraw to SAPIGNIES and to dig in on the right of the village. These lines were commenced about 3.30 am. About 8 am. the Enemy attacked SAPIGNIES from our left and attained the village and about 9 am. the ridge along the left being "in the air", the Battalion withdrew to the BIHUCOURT – SAPIGNIES road, and dug in. Fire was kept up against the Enemy during the withdrawal. At 1.15 pm the Enemy Captured the village of BIHUCOURT and as the left flank of the Bn was threatened at the same time the Battalion withdrew to a line on the reverse slope of the ridge work-west of the BIHUCOURT – SAPIGNIES road. The Battalion withdrew from this line	

WAR DIARY
or
INTELLIGENCE SUMMARY
(Erase heading not required.)

Army Form C. 2118.

Place	Date 1916 March	Hour	Summary of Events and Information	Remarks and references to Appendices
BIEFVOORT	25th		about 2 pm and took up a position in support to the 42nd Division East of LOGEST wood. About 7.0 pm the troops in front withdrew and on orders this Battalion withdrew to the village of GOMMECOURT where it reorganized. Casualties:- Officers wounded, Capt B Hutchinson M.C., 2 Lieut JB DUDDY 5 Cas., wounded & missing; 2/Lt AD MUNRO. Other Ranks killed 8, wounded 46, missing 20. M/D/N. 4. Gas	
GOMMECOURT	26th		At 5.0 am. the Battalion occupies a section of the old enemy front line, prior to 1st July 1916, South of GOMMECOURT wood. This line had been	
do	27th		hit throughout the day which was very quiet. Casualties:- Officers wounded 2/Lt AD PARSONS, wounded 2/Lt J. CARMICHAEL. Other Ranks killed 4, wounded 8 (wounds) 24, missing 2. Gas. At 1.0 am. the Battalion was ordered to withdraw to BIENVILLERS-AU-BOIS. On arrival there about 5 am. the Battalion rested and as per message received the night 27/28 hr the Battalion was ordered at 7.30 am. to "Stand By" to go up the line again and at 1 pm. the Battalion	
BIENVILLERS AU BOIS	28th		moved up to a line East of GOMMECOURT in support to the 42nd Division.	

WAR DIARY or INTELLIGENCE SUMMARY

Place	Date	Hour	Summary of Events and Information	Remarks and references to Appendices
GOMMECOURT	1918 March 28th		Patrols were sent out during night of 28/29 March to get information where troops in front and to clear up the situation round ROSSIGNOL Wood. Otherwise the night & day quiet. Casualties:- Other ranks: killed 1, wounded 2, missing 1. 2/Lt F.W. PALEY, DCM, MM took over duty of Adjutant. The Battalion remained in the sector east of GOMMECOURT till 9 p.m. when it moved up and relieved 1/5th Lancashire Fusiliers in the line in front of BUCQUOY. Relief complete 3.45am 30th. Casualties: Other Ranks, wounded 2.	
—do—	29th			
BUCQUOY	30th		The day passes quietly except for enemy artillery shoot on our front line trenches. Casualties:- Other Ranks killed 2; wounded 15.	
—do—	31st		The Battalion continued to hold the line. Enemy artillery was again active in our front line. Casualties:- Officers ♯ wounded Lt. C.J. RUFFLE, Lt. T. BLACK. Other Ranks killed 6, wounded 19.	

Melvery Craven. Lieut Colonel
Commandy 20th Bn Durham Light Infantry

A P P E N D I C E S   I & II.

SECRET.   20TH BN. DURHAM LIGHT INFANTRY.   COPY NO....
              ORDER NO. 62.

1. **INTENTION.**   The Battalion will entrain from CAMPOSAMPIERO on the
                    2nd and 3rd insts.

2. **INSTRUCTIONS.**
   (a) <u>Times of</u>   C & D Coys. will entrain at 16.39 on the 2nd March.
       <u>Entraining.</u>   A & B Coys. will entrain at 8.39 on the 3rd March.

   (b) <u>Entraining.</u> C Coy. will reach CAMPOSAMPIERO Station at 15.40 and
                    D Coy. at 16.5 on the 2nd inst.
                    A Coy. will reach CAMPOSAMPIERO Station at 7.40, and
                    B Coy. at 8.5 on the 3rd March.
                    Headquarters proceeding on each train will reach the
                    Station with the first company.

   (c) <u>Dress.</u>   Full Marching Order with two blankets.

   (d) <u>Transport.</u> Transport proceeding with the first train will reach
                    the Station by 13.40 on the 2nd inst. Transport
                    proceeding with the second train will be there by
                    5.40 on the 3rd inst.

   (e) <u>Loading.</u>   O.C. A Coy. will detail 3 Officers and 100 men to
                    report to the Transport Officer at the Station at
                    13.40 on the 2nd inst., and at 5.40 pm the 3rd inst.
                    to act as a loading party.

   (f) <u>Officers'</u>   The Officers' Kits and Mess Kits of C & D Coys. <u>not</u>
       <u>Kits and</u>   required on the train will be dumped outside the O.Room
       <u>Mess Kits.</u> by 1.0 p.m. on the 2nd inst.
                    The Officers Kits and Mess Kits of A & B Coys. <u>not</u>
                    required on the train will be dumped outside the O.Room
                    by 10.0 p.m. on the 2nd inst.
                    The Transport Officer will arrange for their collection.
                    All Officers' Kits <u>required</u> for the journey must be
                    taken to the station under Company arrangements.

   (g) <u>Billeting.</u> O's.C. Companies will detail one N.C.O. to report to
                    Lieut. C.J.RUFFLE at 11.0 a.m. tomorrow, 2nd inst.
                    This party will report to the Entraining Officer
                    by 12.30 p.m. and proceed on train No. 21 leaving
                    at 13.39.

3.   ACKNOWLEDGE.

                              (SGD) L.W.SHEPHERDSON,
                                        Lieut. A/Adjutant,
                                    20th Bn. Durham Light Infantry.

1-3-18.
Issued by runner at 5.0 p.m.

Copy No. 1. Filed.   Copy No. 6. O.C. Headquarters
Copy No. 2. O.C. A Coy.   Copy No. 7. Lieut. J.C.R.PACY, M.C
Copy No. 3. O.C. B Coy.   Copy No. 8. Transport Officer.
Copy No. 4. O.C. C Coy.   Copy No. 9. Quartermaster.
Copy No. 5. O.C. D Coy.   Copy No. 10. Medical Officer.
              Copy No. 11 R.S.M.

SECRET.   20TH BN. DURHAM LIGHT INFANTRY.   COPY NO....
          ORDER NO. 64.
          ----

1. **INTENTION**.   The Battalion will proceed by march route, today, to
                SAULTY Station and entrain for the BAISIEUX area.

2. **INSTRUCTIONS**.

(a) Starting   Cross Roads S. end of WARLUZEL.
    POINT.
(b) Time of   1.40 p.m.
    Passing S.P.
(c) Order of   H.Q., B,C,D & A Companies.
    March.
(d) Route.   Road Junction 4/10 Kilos N. of E in COULLEMONT -
                  COUTRELLE - SAULTY.

(e) Halts.   Normal Halts will be observed i.e. the column will halt
                  at 10 minutes to each clock hour and resume the march
                  at the clock hour.

(f) Distances.   A distance of 10 yards will be maintained between Companies.

(g) Formation.   The column will march in three's.

(h) Billets.   All billets must be left scrupulously clean. O's.C. Coys
                  and H.Q. will hand to the Adjutant on parade a
                  certificate to this effect. A certificate will also be
                  handed in at the same time to the effect that all accounts
                  owing from Officers' Mess etc. to the inhabitants have
                  been paid.

(i)   The times given above are subject to alteration by
                  Brigade.

3.   ACKNOWLEDGE.

21-3-18.   (SGD) G.A.BAMLET,
                                          Capt. A/Adjutant.
                                     20th Bn. Durham Light Infantry.

Issued by runner at 9.55 a.m.

Copy No. 1.   Filed.
Copy No. 2.   O.C. A Coy.
Copy No. 3.   O.C. B Coy.
Copy No. 4.   O.C. C Coy.
Copy No. 5.   O.C. D Coy.
Copy No. 6.   Quartermaster.
Copy No. 7.   O.C. Headquarters.
Copy No. 8.   Transport Officer.
Copy No. 9.   War Diary.

41st Division.
124th Infantry Brigade

Came from 123rd Bde. 17.3.18.

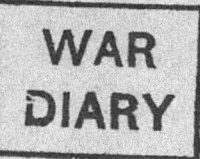

20th BATTALION

THE DURHAM LIGHT INFANTRY

APRIL 1918

Army Form C. 2118.

20th Bn
Durham Light Infantry

WAR DIARY
or
INTELLIGENCE SUMMARY.
(Erase heading not required.)

Place	Date	Hour	Summary of Events and Information	Remarks and references to Appendices
BUCQUOY	April 1st		The Battalion was still holding the line. Enemy artillery was less active than it had been on previous days. There were no casualties to Officers. Other ranks, wounded 2. At 11 PM on night April 1st/2nd the Battn. was relieved by the 1/4th Battn. Lancashire Fusiliers. On completion of relief they proceeded to BIENVILLERS.	
BIENVILLERS	April 2nd		The Battalion then embused for HALLOY at 7AM & on arrival there proceeded to programme of cleaning up as much as possible.	APP. I
HALLOY	April 3rd		At 8.30AM the Battalion proceeded by march route to MONDICOURT & there embused for BONNIERES.	APP. II
BONNIERES	April 4th		During the morning Companies were at the disposal of O.C. Coy for reorganisation etc. At 3.10PM the Battalion entrained from FREVENT STN. (Sidings ground of HOPOUTRE Siding at 9.30PM where it embused for the STEENVORDE area.	
STEENVORDE	April 5th & April 6th		Coys. were at the disposal of Coy Commanders for general reorganisation & reequipping. On April 6th a large draft of (H.S.) 448 O.R.'s arrived & was posted to Coys. Capt J.T. Saunders & 2nd Lieut N. W. Flashell reported from Hospital & were posted to A. Coy full.	
STEENVORDE	April 7th		The Battalion proceeded by march route to the VLAMERTINGHE W. area where they were accommodated in camps.	APP. III

WAR DIARY or INTELLIGENCE SUMMARY

Army Form C. 2118.

Place	Date	Hour	Summary of Events and Information	Remarks and references to Appendices
STEENVOORDE area	April 8th		The Battalion entrained at BRANDHOEK STN. at 9.A.M. & proceeded to ST. JEAN where it detrained & relieved the 1st Battn Border Regt. in Reserve. JYRP	APP. IV
In the line (RESERVE)	April 9th		Companies were at the disposal of Coy Commanders during the day for general re-organisation & specialist training. (NCO?) All four companies were accommodated in cushys. JYRP	
— do —	10th		Training was same as on previous day. A certain percentage of officers reconnoitred all the approaches to the front & support line etc. JYRP	
— do —	11th		Same as on previous day. JYRP	
— do —	12th		Training was carried on as usual in the morning & afternoon. At night the Battn. received a sudden order to move & took up a position in rear of front line & proceeded to dig a line of strong points. The front line became a line of outposts & in consequence was (much?) not so strongly held. JYRP	
— do —	13th		The day passed quietly. The Battn was engaged all day in digging the new line JYRP until nightfall when a composite	
— do —	14th		The digging & wiring of new line was carried on till company composed of platoons of A & C. Coys was left in new line which was to be the new outpost line after the withdrawal of the troops in front. The remainder of the Battalion moved to a position in rear & commenced (the) digging a new line of trenches. These trenches were to be our new Front, Support, & Reserve lines. JYRP	

WAR DIARY
or
INTELLIGENCE SUMMARY.

Army Form C. 2118.

Place	Date	Hour	Summary of Events and Information	Remarks and references to Appendices
In the line	April 15th		Digging & wiring carried on all day & night. Companies relieved one another (afters) each Coy. working for four (4) hours. At night the two platoons of A. Coy on outpost duty were relieved by the two platoons of C. Coy who had been further back digging, thus leaving the whole of C. Coy on outpost duty. JHRP	
– do –	16th		In the early morning the forward outpost line was withdrawn thus (leaving) making the trenches which C. Coy were holding our outpost line. In the afternoon at about 4.30 the enemy, having discovered our withdrawal, were seen advancing over our vacated positions towards our new outpost line. They came to a standstill about 1000 yds from our outpost line. JHRP	
– do –	17th		Day very quiet. Usual work carried out. JHRP	
– do	18th		– do –	
– do	19th		Usual work carried out during day. At night B. Coy relieved C. Coy on outpost duty. C. Coy took up its position in the reserve line. In the early morning the enemy attacked one of our forward posts on Hill 35 causing one or two casualties. Attack was attacked with two platoons, gained our objective but were again driven off. Total casualties 1 Off. missing. 1 Off. wounded & missing. 13 O.Rs missing & 11 O.Rs wounded. JHRP	

WAR DIARY
or
INTELLIGENCE SUMMARY.

(Erase heading not required.)

Army Form C. 2118.

Place	Date	Hour	Summary of Events and Information	Remarks and references to Appendices
In the line	April 20th		Day passed quietly. Usual work carried out. JHRD	
- do -	21st		Companies carried on with digging & wiring as usual. Numerous officers arrived & went back to Companies. One of them has seen service with the Battalion hitherto, viz. in the ST. ELOI sector. LIEUT. A.T. BROWN. Day quite quiet. JHRD	
- do -	22nd 23rd 24th		Usual work carried out uninterruptedly. JHRD On night 24th/25th D. Coy (less one Platoon & 1 Section B. Coy.) look up position on the outpost line. B. Coy was relieved from the outpost line & took up a position in reserve to the remainder of the Battn. JHRD	
- do -	25th		Rather lively day. The enemy shelled our front intermittently all day but did not interfere with the work which was being carried out. JHRD	
- do -	26th		The day passed fairly quietly. At night, beginning at about 9 o'clock, the outpost line withdrew in accordance with instructions to positions on the newly made front line. The Battalion, being relieved from the front line by the new outpost troops, proceeded to YPRES (DEAD END) & occupied a line of trenches in front of DEAD END. which was to become our new front line. JHRD	
- do -	27th		Fairly quiet day. Companies carried out work on the new line. There was a certain amount of hostile shelling probably due to the fact that the enemy had discovered our withdrawal & was following us up. JHRD	

Army Form C. 2118.

WAR DIARY
or
INTELLIGENCE SUMMARY.
(Erase heading not required.)

Instructions regarding War Diaries and Intelligence Summaries are contained in F. S. Regs., Part II. and the Staff Manual respectively. Title pages will be prepared in manuscript.

Place	Date	Hour	Summary of Events and Information	Remarks and references to Appendices
In the line	April 28th		Companies continued with work in the new line of trenches. The morning passed quietly but in the afternoon heavy artillery fire was opened on us to which we replied effectively. Casualties 3 killed & 3 wounded (O.R.'s) J/HB	
- do -	29th		The day passed quietly & companies continued with work on the trenches. J/HB	
- do -	30th		usual work carried on with. Day very quiet. J/HB	

Arthur Hayes. Lieut Col.
Commdg 20th Bn Durham L.I.

7-5-1916.

SECRET.   20TH BN. DURHAM LIGHT INFANTRY   APP. I   COPY NO....
                   ORDER NO. 65.

1. **INTENTION.**   The Battalion will proceed by march route tomorrow,
                       3rd April, to MONDICOURT Church where it will
                       embuss for BONNIERES.

2. **ROUTE.**   Starting Point – GRENAS – MONDICOURT.

3. **STARTING POINT.** 500 yards N.E. of HALLOY on HALLOY – GRENAS Road.

4. **TIME OF PASSING S.P.** Head of the column will pass S.P. at 6.30 a.m.

5. **ORDER OF MARCH.** Headquarters, A, B, C & D Coys.

6. **INTERVALS.**   A distance of 50 yards will be maintained between
                       companies, throughout the march.

7. **BLANKETS.**   Blankets will be rolled in bundles of 10, securely
                       labelled, and taken to the Transport field where they
                       will be loaded on limbers not later than 6.0 a.m.

8. **OFFICERS' VALISES & MESS KITS.** Officers' Valises and Mess Kits will be stacked
                       outside their respective Coy. H.Q. by 6.15 a.m.
                       The Transport Officer will arrange to collect them.

9. **TRANSPORT.**   The Transport, less 4 cookers and 1 water-cart, will
                       be formed up on HALLOY – LUCHEUX Road with head of
                       the column on the South Side of l'Esperance X Roads
                       at 9.30 a.m. tomorrow, 3rd inst., whence it will march
                       to BONNIERES under the orders of the Brigade Transport
                       Officer. Mess Cart, 4 cookers and 1 water-cart will
                       leave HALLOY at 7.30 a.m. on 3rd inst., and proceed
                       by march route via LUCHEUX – BOUQUEMAISON – ARBRAS MON
                       LERLOND to BONNIERES, where they will wait at the
                       Church until guides from the Battalion arrive to
                       show them where billets are situated. They will
                       cook on the road so as to be able to serve a hot meal
                       to the troops on arrival at billets.

10. **BILLETING.**   A Billeting Party of 1 N.C.O. per Company and 1 from
                       H.Q. will parade under 2/Lieut. A. GRAHAM at Battn.
                       Orderly Room at 6.15 a.m. They will meet Brigade
                       Billeting Officer at BONNIERES Church at 9.30 a.m.
                       3rd inst. They will meet the Battalion at
                       BONNIERES and guide Companies to their billets on
                       arrival. They will also provide a guide for the c
                       cookers and water-cart to show them where Companies
                       are billeted.

11. **ACKNOWLEDGE.**

                                   (SGD)   F.W. PALEY,
                                           2/Lieut. A/Adjutant,
2-4-1918.   20th Bn. Durham Light Infantry.

Issued by runner at 10.15 p.m.

Copies to:-

No. 1. FILED.   No. 5. O.C. D Coy.
No. 2. O.C. A Coy.   No. 6. Q.M. & T.O.
No. 3. O.C. B Coy.   No. 7. O.C. Headquarters.
No. 4. O.C. C Coy.   No. 8. R.S.M.

SECRET.   20TH BN. DURHAM LIGHT INFANTRY. APP II COPY NO....
                 ENTRAINING ORDERS.
----

1. The Battalion will entrain tomorrow, 4th April, 1918, at
   FREVENT STATION. Time of departure - 3.20 p.m.
   Train No. 17 will be composed of this Battalion and 124 Light
   Trench Mortar Battery.

2. Companies will parade at 1.20 p.m. with the head of the column
   opposite Headquarter"s Mess.
   Order of March - Headquarters, B,C,D & A Coys.

3. Blankets, rolled in bundles of 10 and <u>securely labelled</u>, will
   be carried to the Transport Lines where they will be loaded
   on limbers by 11.0 a.m.
   Officers' Valises and Mess Kits will be carried to the
   Transport Lines and loaded by 11.0 a.m.

4. The Transport will report at FREVENT Station at 12.20 p.m.
   The 19th Bn. Middlesex Regt. are providing a loading party.
   The Supply and Baggage Wagons attached to this unit will
   entrain loaded, with the Battalion.
   There will be an ambulance at the entraining and detraining
   stations.

5. Company Commanders will warn all ranks against leaving the train
   without permission. Such application must be made to the
   Commanding Officer.

6. A distance of 50 yards will be maintained between Companies
   on the march.

7. <u>ACKNOWLEDGE</u>.

                          (SGD) F.W.PALEY,
                                 2/Lieut. A/Adjutant,
3-4-18.   20TH Bn. Durham Light Infantry.

Issued by runner at 8.15 p.m.

Copies to:-

No. 1. Filed.   No. 5. O.C. D Coy.
No. 2. O.C. A Coy.   No. 6. Q.m. & T.O.
No. 3. O.C. B Coys   No. 7. O.C. Headquarters.
No. 4. O.C. C Coys   No. 8. R.S.M.

SECRET.   20TH BN. DURHAM LIGHT INFANTRY.   APP. IV   COPY NO....

                                                   APP. III

SECRET.   20TH BN. DURHAM LIGHT INFANTRY.   COPY NO...
               ORDER NO. 66.

1. INTENTION..   The Battalion will move to the VLAMERTINGHE Area, today, 7th inst.

2. STARTING POINT.   The fork roads just S. of H.Q. Men's Billet.

3. TIME OF PASSING S.P.   10.0 a.m.

4. ROUTE.   STEENVOORDE – ABEELE – POPERINGHE – VLAMERTINGHE.

5. ORDER OF MARCH.   Headquarters, C, D, A & B Coys., Transport.

6. BLANKETS.   Blankets, rolled in bundles of 10 and securely labelled, will be stacked by Companies on the nearest main road leading to STEENVOORDE by 8.0 a.m. All men with bad feet and unable to march should be used as a guard over the blankets and will travel with them on the lorry.

7. OFFICERS' KITS & MESS KITS.   All Officers' Valises and Mess Kits will be dumped with the blankets and should be ready for collection by 8.30 a.m.
Each Company and H.Q. will send a man to the Transport Lines to guide Transport to the place where kits etc. have been dumped.
One man per Company and H.Q. will also report to the Quartermaster at H.Q. Men's Billet to act as guide for lorry. These guides should report not later than 8.0 a.m. The lorry allotted to this Battalion can be used all day. One Headquarter Runner will report to Brigade H.Q. at 8.0 a.m. today, to guide the lorry to Headquarter Men's Billet.

8. RELIEF.   The Battalion will relieve a Battalion of the 29th Division in the Right Brigade Sector of the Left Division, VIIIth Corps, on the night of the 9/10th April, 1918. An Advance Party will remain behind in this area until 5.30 p.m. today, 7th April, at which hour they will report to Brigade H.Q., WINNEZEELE. A lorry will convey this party from Brigade H.Q. to the Forward Area and they will live with their opposite numbers in the Line until the Battalion moves into the Line. This party will consist of Lieut. L.W. SHEPHERDSON, M.C., 1 Officer, 1 N.C.O. and 2 runners per Company. Rations for the 9th inst. will be carried.

9. BILLETING PARTY.   A Billeting Party consisting of 2/Lieut. N.W. Turnbull and 1 N.C.O. from each Company and H.Q. will meet the Staff Captain at Brigade H.Q., WINNEZEELE at 6.0 a.m. today, 7th inst.

10. DISTANCES.   The following distances will be maintained on the line of march:-
       500 yards between Battalions.
       100 yards between Companies.
        50 yards between each group of 6 vehicles.

11. TRANSPORT.   All First Line Transport will accompany the Battalion.

12. ACKNOWLEDGE.

                        (SGD) F.W. PALEY,
                              2/Lieut. A/Adjutant,
7th April, 1918.   20th Bn. Durham Light Infantry.

SECRET.   20TH BN. DURHAM LIGHT INFANTRY.   APP. IV   COPY NO....
               ORDER NO. 67.
               ----

1. **INTENTION.**   The Battalion will relieve the 1st Bn. Border Regt. 67th Inf. Bde. in the Reserve Line today, 8th April, 1918.

2. **ENTRAINMENT.** The Battalion will entrain at BRANDHOEK Station at 9.0 a.m. today. Companies will march independently and will reach the station at 8.30 a.m. At least one guide per Company should be sent on ahead to reconnoitre the approaches to the station. Companies will detrain at ST. JEAN and C Coy. will then march to CALIFORNIA Camp and relieve a Company of the 1st Border Regt.

3. **TRENCH STORES ETC.** All aeroplane photographs, Defence Schemes, Maps, S.A.A., Grenades, Trench Stores including Reserve Rations, Policy of Work and Intelligence Notes will be taken over and lists forwarded to this office by 9.0 a.m., 9th inst.

4. **COMPLETION OF RELIEF.** Completion of relief will be reported to this Office, by special runner.

5. **BLANKETS, OFFICERS' KITS & MESS KITS.** All blankets rolled in bundles of 10 and labelled will be stacked as follows:-
   A & B Coys. at Transport Lines.
   C & D Coys. - Close to the road near Headquarter & H.Q. Officers' Quarters.
   All Mess Kit and Officers' Valises will be dumped at the same place.
   All the above must be dumped at 7.15 a.m.

6. **LEWIS GUNS.** All Lewis Guns will be taken to the new quarters on limbers and delivered to Companies.

7. **TRANSPORT.** All cookers, water-carts and other vehicles conveying kit etc. will move to the new camps under arrangements made with the Transport Officer. One of the water-carts should report to C Coy. at CALIFORNIA Camp.
   The Transport of the Battalion will move to REIGERSURG Camp today, 8th inst., and will take over the Lines of the 1st Border Regt. at 2.0 p.m.

8. **ACKNOWLEDGE.**

                                    (SGD) F.W.PALEY,
                                          2/Lieut. A/Adjutant,
8th April, 1918.   20th Bn. Durham Light Infantry.
Issued by runner at 2.45 a.m.

Copies to:-
No. 1. Filed.   No. 7. O.C. Headquarters.
No. 2. O.C. A Coy.   No. 8. Medical Officer.
No. 3. O.C. B Coy.   No. 9. Transport Officer.
No. 4. O.C. C Coy.   No. 10. Quartermaster.
No. 5. O.C. D Coy.   No. 11. R.S.M.
No. 6. 2nd in Command.

Army Form C. 2118.

WAR DIARY
or
INTELLIGENCE SUMMARY.   20th Bn. Durham. L.I.

(Erase heading not required.)

Place	Date	Hour	Summary of Events and Information	Remarks and references to Appendices
In the line	1/5/18		During the day everybody rested as far as possible. At night working parties were busy on a new outpost line which was to be occupied in the event of a further withdrawal on our part.	JYRP
- do -	2/5/18		Companies rested during the day. At night [crossed out] the Battalion was relieved by the 15th Hants. & proceeded to a camp near VLAMERTINGHE where they & the rest of the Brigade went to be in Divisional Reserve.	JYRP
In camp	3/5/18		Companies rested during the morning. In the afternoon worked on a new line which was to be fallen back on if a further withdrawal was being dug. This line was to be became necessary.	JYRP
- do -	4/5/18		The usual working parties were busy on the new line of trenches in the afternoon. In the morning specialists trained under their respective officers	JYRP
- do -	5/5/18		Being Sunday voluntary Church services were held. The working parties carried on as usual in the afternoon.	JYRP
- do -	6/5/18		Specialist training only in the morning. The new line of trenches was further improved. Companies worked under R.E supervision.	JYRP
- do -	7/5/18		Specialist training only in morning & afternoon. New line of trenches further enlarged under R.E supervision.	

WAR DIARY
INTELLIGENCE SUMMARY.

(Erase heading not required.)

Army Form C. 2118.

Instructions regarding War Diaries and Intelligence Summaries are contained in F. S. Regs., Part II. and the Staff Manual respectively. Title pages will be prepared in manuscript.

Place	Date	Hour	Summary of Events and Information	Remarks and references to Appendices
In Camp	8/5/18		Specialist training in morning and afternoon. New line of trenches further improved by Companies under R.E. supervision.	—
— do —	9/5/18		Special training in morning + afternoon. New line of trenches further improved by Companies under R.E. supervision.	—
— do —	10/5/18		Special training in morning + afternoon. New line of trenches further improved by Companies under R.E. supervision. Advance parties proceeded at night to reconnoitre line.	—
— do —	11/5/18		Inspection of Companies by Company Commanders. — Preparation for relief. Relieved 3 Companies of 1st Bn K.S.L.I. and one Company 1st West Yorks in the morning.	APP 1
In the line	12/5/18		During day everyone rested as much as possible. Working parties + patrols were busy during the night. Situation during the day was normal.	—
— do —	13/5/18		During day everyone rested as much as possible — working parties + patrols were busy during the night. Situation during day was normal.	—
— do —	14/5/18		During day everyone rested as much as possible — Working parties and patrols were busy during the night. The weather was fine during the day — Observation good — One of our patrols captured a soldier of the 458th I.R.	—
— do —	15/5/18		During day everyone rested as much as possible — the weather during the day was fine — Observation good — there is new disposition in front line took place. "D" Coy was relieved by a Coy of the 10th Queens Royal West Surrey Regiment (in skeleton).	—

WAR DIARY
INTELLIGENCE SUMMARY

Army Form C. 2118.

Place	Date	Hour	Summary of Events and Information	Remarks and references to Appendices
In the Line	16/5/18	—	During the day everyone rested as much as possible. The weather during the day was good – Observation good – Working parties were busy improving trenches during the night. Patrols were active.	Hrs
— do —	18/5/18	—	During the day everyone rested as much as possible. The weather during the day was fine – Observation good – Working parties were busy improving trenches during the night. Our patrols were active. Enemy activity much increased.	Hrs
— do —	19/5/18	—	During the day everyone rested as much as possible. Weather fine – Observation good – ~~Working parties were busy~~ At night the Battalion was relieved by the 10th Queens Royal West Surrey Regt. and proceeded by tramlines to the following disposition. "A" Coy Bolle House Line "D" Coy Grand Street APP II to "C" Coy to V.12. 6 by 6 , V.13 – 13 H.Q. at V1 where the Battalion were in Bivouac areas.	Hrs / APP II
— do —	20/5/18	—	During the day everyone rested as much as possible – Weather fine – Observation good – Working parties were busy during the night.	Hrs
— do —	21/5/18	—	During the day everyone rested as much as possible – Weather fine – Observation good – Working parties were busy during the night.	Hrs

Army Form C. 2118.

WAR DIARY
or
INTELLIGENCE SUMMARY.

20th Durham L.I.

(Erase heading not required.)

Instructions regarding War Diaries and Intelligence Summaries are contained in F. S. Regs, Part II. and the Staff Manual respectively. Title pages will be prepared in manuscript.

Place	Date	Hour	Summary of Events and Information	Remarks and references to Appendices
In the Line	22/5/18		The Battalion rested during the day and sapplied working parties at night. Weather very hot.	
"	23/5/18		As above. Weather exceedingly hot.	
"	24/5/18		As above. Weather dull and cooler.	
"	25/5/18		The Battalion was relieved by the 15th Royal Hampshire Regt and marched to BRAKE CAMP as part of the Brigade in Reserve. Baths were provided for all the Battalion and the men afterwards rested. Service was held by the C of E. and for Catholics & other denominations	APP III
"	27/5/18		Owing to an Enemy attack the Battalion was called out and occupied an assembly position from 10:30 am to 6.30 pm. When they returned to Camp B.	
"	28/5/18		The Battalion supplied working parties for rear positions. Lewis Gunners remained in Camp for training. Weather very fine.	

WAR DIARY
or
INTELLIGENCE SUMMARY.

Army Form C. 2118.

20th Durham L.I.

Place	Date	Hour	Summary of Events and Information	Remarks and references to Appendices
BRAKE Camp	29/5/18		The Battalion spent the whole day training, under its respective Company Commanders and Specialist Officers. Weather very fine.	
Do	30/5/18		As above	
Do	31/5/18		As above	

2-6-18.

Aubrey Grey(?) Lieut. Col.,
Commdg. 20th Bn. Durham L.I.

APPENDIX. 1.

SECRET.   20TH BN. DURHAM LIGHT INFANTRY.   COPY NO...
                 ORDER NO. 68.
                 ----

1. **INTENTION.**   The Battalion will relieve part of the 16th Inf. Bde.
                     and part of the 18th Inf. Bde. in the line on the
                     night of the 11th May, 1918.

2. **ORDER OF**   A Coy. D.L.I. will relieve B Coy. 1st K.S.L.I.
   RELIEF.   B "   "   "   "   "   D "   "   "
                     D "   "   "   "   "   C "   "   "
                     C "   "   "   "   "   C "   1st West Yorks.

3. **GUIDES.**   1 Guide for Battn.H.Q., 1 for Coy H.Q. and 1 per
                     platoon will meet the Battalion at X Roads, H.10.b.35.30.
                     at 8.30 p.m.

4. **INTERVALS.**   Companies will move independently, commencing at 7.45 p.m.
                     in the order B,A,C, D, Headqarters, with 5 minutes
                     interval between platoons.

5. **TRENCH**   Company Commanders will take over all details of the
   STORES.   Defence Scheme from the Company they are relieving,
                     also all Trench Stores, Aeroplane Photographs, Plans
                     of Work etc. Lists of all stores taken over will be
                     forwarded to this office by noon, 12th inst.

6. **LEWIS GUNS.**   Companies will each take 4 Lewis Guns, 20 magazines
                     per Gun and spare part bags into the line.

7. **DRESS.**   Battle Order with great-coats.

8. **TRANSPORT.**   All Officers' valises, surplus mess kits, packs,
                     blankets, Lewis Guns, Magazines etc. not reQired for
                     the line, will be stacked outside Battn. Orderly Room
                     by 7.0 p.m.
                     All trench bundles, Mess Kits etc. required for the line
                     will be stacked in Company lines ready for loading
                     at 7.0 p.m.
                     1 limber per Company and 1 for H.Qrs. will convey
                     Lewis Guns, Trench Bundles etc. to the line.
                     Company Commanders will use their discretion as to the
                     off-loading point. The Transport Officer will arrange
                     for the above mentioned transport.

9. **DETAILS.**   The undermentioned personnel will not proceed in to
                     the line:-
                          Major C. PANNAL, M.C.
                          Lieut. G.H. JOHNSON.
                          R.S.M.
                          5 O.R. from each Company for Instructional Class
                          20 Signallers as detailed by the Signalling Officer

10. **COMPLETION**   Completion of Relief will be reported to Bn. H.Q. by
    OF RELIEF.   wiring "NIL LEAVE RETURN".

11.   ACKNOWLEDGE.

                                  (SGD) F.W. PALEY,
                                         Capt. & Adjutant,
11-5-1918.   20th Bn. Durham Light Infantry.
Issued by runner at 12 noon.

Copies to:-
          No. 1. Filed.   No. 6. Major C.PANNALL, M.C.
          No. 2. O.C. A Company.   No. 7. Signalling Officer.
          No. 3. O.C. B Company.   No. 8. Medical Officer.
          No. 4. O.C. C Company.   No. 9. Q.M. & T.O.
          No. 5. O.C. D Company.

APPENDIX II

SECRET.   20TH BN. DURHAM LIGHT INFANTRY.   COPY NO...
ORDER NO. 69.

1. The Battalion will be relieved on night of 19th/20th May, 1918, by the 10th Bn. "Queens" R.W.S. Regt.

   B Coy. "Queens" will relieve C Coy. D.L.I.
   C   "   "   "   A   "   "
   D   "   "   "   B   "   "
   A   "   "   "   D   "   "

2. Advance Parties of 1 Officer and 4 Other Ranks from the "Queens" are reporting to Companies tonight.

3. Guides will be found by the "Queens" for their Advance Parties.

4. All plans of Work, Trench Stores etc. will be handed over on relief and the usual receipts obtained and forwarded to this office by 12 noon, 21st inst.

5. On relief the Battalion will move into reserve and will be distributed as follows:-
   A Coy. - DOLLS HOUSE LINE.
   D COY. - CANAL SWITCH.
   C &
   B Coys.- GOLDFISH CHATEAU AREA.
   H.Q.   - H.18.a.0.7.

6. Rations limbers will be met by 2 guides from each Coy's Advance Party at Battalion H.Q. (H.18.a.0.7.).
   These guides will take ration limbers to a point as close to Coy. H.Qrs. as possible, where rations will be dumped. One man will act as guard over these rations and the other will proceed to Company H.Q. to act as a guide to the Ration Party.
   Advance Parties have been given full instructions.

7. Completion of Relief will be reported to this office by wiring " YOUR S 100 RECEIVED".
   Companies will also wire name of Company Commander when they have settled in their new positions.

8. Companies will arrange to carry out kit, trench bundles etc. to the new positions.

9. ACKNOWLEDGE.

(SGD) F.W. PALEY,

Capt. & Adjutant,
19-5-18.   20th Bn. Durham Light Infantry.

Issued by runner at 2.0 a.m.

Copy No. 1. FILED.
  " No. 2. O.C. A Coy.
  " No. 3. O.C. B Boy.
  " No. 4. O.C. C Coy.
  " No. 5. O.C. D Coy.
  " No. 6. O.C. Headquarters.

APPENDIX....

SECRET.   20TH BN. DURHAM LIGHT INFANTRY.   COPY NO....
                           ORDER NO. 70.
                 ----

1.   The Battalion will be relieved by the 15th Bn. HANTS Regt. on night of 25th/26th May, 1918.

2.   C Coy.   HANTS will relieve   A Coy.   D.L.I.
     B   "   "   "   "   B   "   "
     A   C   "   "
     D   D   "   "

3.   On relief Companies will move independently, by platoons at 200 yds. interval, to BRAKE CAMP - A.30.c.6.1. via PLANK Road on N. side of YPRES - VLAMERTINGHE Road.

4.   An Advance Party consisting of 1 Officer, 1 N.C.O. and 2 runners per Company of the incoming Unit, will report to Companies tonight, 24th inst.

5.   1 N.C.O. per Company and 1 N.C.O. from H.Qrs. will report to Lieut. L.W.SHEPHERDSON, M.C., at Bn. H.W. at 9.0 am. tomorrow, 25th inst.
     Full equipment will be carried.
     This N.C.O. will meet his Company on the PLANK Road about 500 yds N.W. of VLAMERTINGHE, at a time to be arranged by Company Commanders, and guide the Company to BRAKE CAMP.

6.   1 Guide per platoon, 1 guide from each Coy. H.Q. and 1 from Bn. H.Qrs. will report at these H.Qrs. at 9.0 p.m. tomorrow, 25th inst.
     O's.C. Companies must give to their guides full instructions as to which Companies of the relieving Unit they are to meet.

7.   Companies will hand over details of Defence Schemes, Work in Progress, Trench Stores, S.O.S. Grenades, and 10 Petrol Tins per Coy.
     Duplicate kisix receipts will be obtained and forwarded to this office by 6.0 p.m., 26th inst.

8.   1 limber per Company and 1 for H.Qrs. will report at the respective ration dumps as under:-

          H.Qrs   -   10.0 p.m.
          B & C Coys. -   11.30 p.m.
          A & D Coys. -   11.45 p.m.

9.   Companies will send any kit etc. not required tomorrow, down by empty ration limbers tonight.

10. Completion of Relief will be notified to this Office by wiring "YOUR G.50 RECEIVED".

11. ACKNOWLEDGE.

                              (SGD) F.W. PALEY,
                                           Capt. & Adjutant,
24-5-18.   20th Bn. Durham Light Infantry.

Issued by runner at 9.30 p.m.

Copy No. 1.   FILED.
  " No. 2.   O.C. A Coy.
  " No. 3.   O.C. B Coy.
  " No. 4.   O.C. C Coy.
  " No. 5.   O.C. D Coy.
  " No. 6.   Q.M. & T.O.
  " No. 7.   O.C. 15th HANTS.
  " No. 8.   Lieut. L.W.SHEPHERDSON, M.C.

20 DL1 Army Form C. 2118.

WAR DIARY

~~INTELLIGENCE SUMMARY~~

(Erase heading not required.)

Instructions regarding War Diaries and Intelligence Summaries are contained in F.S. Regs., Part II. and the Staff Manual respectively. Title pages will be prepared in manuscript.

Place	Date 1918 June	Hour	Summary of Events and Information	Remarks and references to Appendices
In Camp	1st		Specialist & Platoon training was carried out as per programme. Commanding Officer inspected B & C Companies in the afternoon.	Nil
do	2nd		Voluntary Divine Services were held in the morning & evening	Nil
do	3rd		The Battalion moved from BRAKE CAMP (on being relieved by 1st-7th Batt. Yorks) APP.I by light railway to PROVEN & thence to WATTEN by broad gauge - moving by march route to billets near LEDERZEELE	Nil
In Battalion	4th		General cleaning of equipment & billets in the morning - In the afternoon training under platoon commanders was carried out	Nil
do	5th		During the day Companies were at the disposal of O.C. Corps specialists under specialist officers. In the evening an Officers' Riding class was commenced.	Nil
do	6th		Training was carried out as per programme. - Officers' Riding class	Nil
do	7th		Training was carried out as per programme - Officers' Riding class in the evening and an inter-company long distance run was held	Nil

Army Form C. 2118.

WAR DIARY
INTELLIGENCE SUMMARY.
(Erase heading not required.)

Instructions regarding War Diaries and Intelligence Summaries are contained in F. S. Regs., Part II. and the Staff Manual respectively. Title pages will be prepared in manuscript.

Place	Date 1918 JUNE	Hour	Summary of Events and Information	Remarks and references to Appendices
In billets	8th		Rifle Range allotted to A, B & D companies in the morning — O.C. Divl. train inspected the transport — In the afternoon the Battalion moved by march route to billets at Bonningues-lez-Ardres	
— do —	9th		Voluntary Divine Service were held in the evening	
— do —	10th		Morning — Companies at disposal of O.sC. for kit inspection, cleaning of equipment, ammunition & Lewis Guns. Afternoon — Rifle Range allotted to B & C Coys. A & D Coys. carried out tactical training	
— do —	11th		Companies carried out tactical training under Coy Commanders. Lecture by Brigade Commander at 5.30 pm to all Officers & N.C.Os.	
— do —	12th		Rifle Range was allotted to A & D companies in the morning & B & C Coys. in the afternoon. Divisional Baths at CLERQUES were allotted to Battn. Lecture to Officers by Divil. Commander.	
— do —	13th		The Battalion carried out a tactical scheme on training area	
— do —	14th		The Battalion took part in a Brigade attack scheme	
— do —	15th		"B" Company carried out firing practices on the range. A, C & D Companies training & musketry	

Army Form C. 2118.

WAR DIARY
or
INTELLIGENCE SUMMARY.
(Erase heading not required.)

Place	Date 1918 June	Hour	Summary of Events and Information	Remarks and references to Appendices
In Lillers	16th		Voluntary divine services were held during the day	Ref.
— do —	17th.		Companies carried out training according to programme. Company Sports were held in the evening.	Ref.
— do —	18th.		The Battalion took part in a Brigade attack Scheme in training area.	Ref.
— do —	19th.		During the day range firing & bathing was carried out on Andrelun Range and at Blargues Baths.	Ref.
— do —	20th.		Companies carried out inter-company attack schemes in training area. A Company held sports in the evening	Ref.
— do —	21st		The Battalion carried out an attack scheme on training area.	Ref.
— do —	22nd		The Battalion were inspected in the morning by the Brigade Commander. and in the afternoon by the Brigade Bombardier.	Ref.
— do —	23rd		Voluntary divine services were held during the day.	Ref.

Army Form C. 2118.

WAR DIARY
or
INTELLIGENCE SUMMARY.
(Erase heading not required.)

Instructions regarding War Diaries and Intelligence Summaries are contained in F. S. Regs., Part II. and the Staff Manual respectively. Title pages will be prepared in manuscript.

Place	Date 1918 JUNE	Hour	Summary of Events and Information	Remarks and references to Appendices
In billets	24th		During the day companies carried out training on training area	Ref.
— do —	25th		The Battalion moved to billets in LEDERZEELE area. by march route	APP IV Ref.
— do —	26th		The Battalion moved by march route to billets in OUDEZEELE area.	Ref.
— do —	27th		Companies carried out kit inspections, respirator inspections, general cleaning of arms, equipment & ammunition.	Ref.
— do —	28th		Companies carried out training on drill during the day, instruction on their own weapons — Reconnoitring parties proceeded to the Bois de la Line	Ref.
— do —	29th		The Battalion moved by march route to billets at ABEELE. Advance parties proceeded to the trenches in the vicinity of KEMMEL.	APP IV Ref.
— do —	30th		The Battalion relieved a Battalion of French 102 R.I. in the vicinity of KEMMEL on night 30th June – 1st July	APP V Ref.

Channell Major
Comm'g 20th Bn Durham L.I.

APPENDIX I

SECRET.   20TH BN. DURHAM LIGHT INFANTRY.   COPY NO....
                                    ORDER NO. 71.

1. **INTENTION.** The Battalion will be relieved by the 1/7th Bn. West York Regt. tomorrow, 3rd June, 1918, and, on completion of relief will proceed to HAGLE DUMP (Sheet 28 N.W. - G.6 Central) where it will entrain in the Light Railway for PUGWASH, thence proceeding to the Second Army Training Area by Tactical Train, for which move instructions will be issued later.

2. **TIME OF STARTING.** Companies will "Stand to" from 8 a.m. ready to move off independently immediately O's.C.Companies have handed over to the incoming unit.

3. **ENTRAINING.** Major C. PANNALL, M.C., will superintend the entraining of the Battalion. Trains are allotted as under:-
   Train No. 1 - A & B Companies.
   "   " 2 - C & D   "
   "   " 3 - Headquarters and Details.

4. **BILLETING PARTY.** A Billeting Party, consisting of 2/Lieut. J. TERRY, one N.C.O. per Coy., and 2 from H.Q., will be held in readiness to proceed by cycle to the final destination immediately on receipt of instructions.

5. **TRANSPORT ARRANGEMENTS.** Officers' Kits will be dumped outside Orderly Room by 6.30 a.m. tomorrow for collection by a G.S.Wagon. Lewis Gun Limbers and Field Kitchens will report to Companies at the same time and must be loaded immediately.
   Officers' Mess Kits not arranged for in My S.26/280 of today's date will travel on the Field Kitchen.

6. **TRANSPORT.** Transport will proceed by March Route to the New Area in accordance with instructions to be issued later and will arrive at the final destination on the 4th inst.

7. **DRESS.**   FULL MARCHING ORDER.

8. **AREA STORES.** All Area Stores etc., Ammunition in Camp, excepting 120 rounds per man and Lewis Gun Ammunition, and petrol tins surplus to those carried on the 1st line Transport will be handed over to the incoming unit and the receipt forwarded to these Headquarters.
   O's.C. Companies will obtain a certificate from their opposite number to the effect that their portion of the camp has been handed over in a thoroughly clean and sanitary condition. This certificate must be forwarded as early as possible.

9. **ACKNOWLEDGE.**

                                    (SGD) L.W.SHEPHERDSON, Lieut., Asst. Adjt.,
2nd June, 1918.   20th Bn. Durham Light Infantry.
Issued by runner at 5 p.m.

Copies to:-
No. 1 Filed.
No. 2. O.C. A Company.
No. 3. O.C. B Company.
No. 4. O.C. C Company.
No. 5. O.C. D Company.
No. 6. Major C. PANNALL, M.C.
No. 7. Medical Officer.
No. 8. Quartermaster.
No. 9. Transport Officer.
No. 10. R.S.M.

APPENDIX II

SECRET. 20TH BN. DURHAM LIGHT INFANTRY. COPY NO....
ORDER NO. 72.

1. **INTENTION.** The Battalion will proceed by March Route to the BONNINGUE Area today, June 8th, 1918.

2. **ROUTE.** WATTEN - GANSPETTE - BAYENGHEM - NORDAUSQUES - TOURNEHEM - BONNINGUES.

3. **STARTING POINT.** Les 5 Rues (HAZEBROUCK 5A)

4. **ORDER OF MARCH.** Headquarters, A,B,C & D Coys., Transport.

5. **TIME OF PASSING S.P.**
    - Headquarters - 3-30 p.m.
    - A Company - 3-31 p.m.
    - B Company - 3-32 p.m.
    - C Company - 3-33 p.m.
    - D Company - 3-34 p.m.
    - Transport - 3-35 p.m.

6. **TRANSPORT.** Lewis Gun Limbers will report to Companies forthwith.

7. **OFFICERS' KITS.** Officers' Kits will be dumped outside Company H.Q. as soon as possible.

8. **OFFICERS' MESS KITS.** Officers' Mess Kits will travel on the Field Kitchens.

9. **RATIONS.** Rations for tomorrow, now in possession of Companies will also be carried on the Field Kitchens.

10. **TEAS.** Teas will be served on arrival in the New Area.

11. **AREA STORES.** All tents will be struck and dumped in the field behind the Q.M. Stores.
    Number of tents dumped will be reported to this Office.
    Ablution bowls will also be dumped there.
    The present Battalion Guard will remain behind in charge of this dump.

12. **DISTANCES.** The following distances will be maintained on the march:-
    100 yards between Companies.
    100 yards between rear Company and Transport.

13. **ACKNOWLEDGE.**

(SGD) L.W.SHEPHERDSON, Lieut.Asst.Adjt.
20th Bn. Durham Light Infantry.

8th June, 1918.
Issued by runner at 2.40 p.m.
Copies to: 1

No. 1 Filed.
No. 2. O.C. A Company.
No. 3. O.C. B Company.
No. 4. O.C. C Company.
No. 5. O.C. D Company.
No. 6. Major C.PANNALL, M.C.
No. 7. Quartermaster.
No. 8. Transport Officer.
No. 9. R.S.M.

APPENDIX III

SECRET.   20TH BN. DURHAM LIGHT INFANTRY ORDER NO.73.   Copy No...

Ref. Map - HAZEBROUCK 5A.

1. **INTENTION.** The Battalion will move to the CROME STRAETE (LEDERZEELE Area) tomorrow, 25th June 1918, by march route. Transport will accompany the Battalion.

2. **STARTING POINT.**
Level Crossing East of BONNINGUES on BONNINGUES - TOURNEHEM ROAD.

3. **TIME OF PASSING S.P.**
Coys. will be in position with the head of the column at the S.P. by 8.50 a.m.

4. **ORDER OF MARCH.**
H.Q., B,C,D,A Coy, Transport.

5. **INTERVALS.** The following distances will be maintained on the march:-
100 yards between Companies.
100 yards between rear Coy. and Transport.
Gaps of 25 yards will be left between every 6 vehicles.

6. **HALTS.** The normal halts at 10 minutes before every clock hour will be observed. There will be a long halt for dinners at 11.50 a.m. and the march will be resumed at 1 p.m.

7. **BILLETING PARTY.**
2/Lieut. J.TERRY, one N.C.O. from H.Q. and one per Coy. will report to the Area Commandnat, LEDERZEELE at 7 a.m. tomorrow. The party will rendezvous at 5 a.m. at Orderly Room where bicycles will be provided. As far as possible the billets previously occupied in this area will be taken over.

8. **OFFICERS' VALISES & MESS KITS.**
Valises will be stacked outside the respective Headquarters by 7.30 a.m. Mess Kits will be stacked at the same place by 8 a.m.

9. **LEWIS GUNS.** Companies will arrange to load Lewis Gun Limbers in the Transport Lines by 8 a.m.

10. **LORRIES.** One lorry will report at Bn. H.Q. at 8 a.m. It will remain with the Battalion until the night of the 26th inst. and will make as many journeys as are necessary. As far as possible the lorry must be sent by a different route to the troops.

11. **SICK.** An ambulance will follow in rear of the Brigade.

12. **RATIONS.** Rations for consumption on the 26th inst. will be delivered in the new area.

13. **AREA STORES ETC.**
All tents, wash basins and urine pails etc. issued from the Orderly Room as Area Stores will be returned to this office by 7.30 a.m. All surplus Practice S.A.A. and Grenades will be handed over to the Billet Warden by the Q.M. and a statement of the amount handed over forwarded to this office on arrival in the new area.

14. **RUNNERS.** One runner per Coy. will be sent to report to Battn. H.Q. on arrival at CROME STRAETE.

15. **ROUTE FOR MARCH.**
TOURNEHEM - NORDAUSQUES - BAYENGHEM - EST MONT - WATTEN - X Roads at LE BERSTACKE.

16. **BILLETS.** All billets will be left in a clean and sanitary condition and a certificate rendered to this effect by O'sC. Coys. on arrival in the new area.

17. ACKNOWLEDGE.

24th June 1918.   (SGD) F.W.PALEY. Capt. Adjutant.
Issued by runner at 11.20 p.m.
Copies to:-   No. 1 Filed.   No. 6 2nd in Command.
              No. 2 O.C. A Coy. No. 7 T.O. & Q.M.
              No. 3 O.C. B Coy. No. 8 Medical Officer.
              No. 4 O.C. C Coy. No. 9 R.S.M.
              No. 5 O.C. D Coy.

App.4

SECRET. 20TH BN. DURHAM LIGHT INFANTRY Copy No....
ORDER NO. 75.

Reference Map - Sheet 27.

1. **INTENTION.** The Battalion will move to "Z" Area (near ABEELE) today, 29th June 1918.

2. **STARTING POINT.** Road opposite B Coy's Billet at J.31.b.4.0.

3. **TIME OF PASSING S.P.** Head of Column will pass S.P. at 5 p.m.

4. **ORDER OF MARCH.** Headquarters, D,A,B,C Coy.

5. **ROUTE.** S.P. - Junction of Road with main CASSELL - STEENVOORDE Road just S. of the 2 in Square 2 - STEENVOORDE - ABEELE - Thence to bivouacs in O.32 & 33.

6. **INTERVALS.** Until STEENVOORDE is reached the usual distances will be maintained between Companies. East of STEENVOORDE platoons will move at 100 yards distance and should keep well into the right side of the road so as to obtain the maximum of cover afforded by the screen.

7. **OFFICERS' VALISES.** Officers' Valises will be stacked outside the respective Company H.Q. by 4 p.m.

8. **TEAS.** Teas will be served before moving off.

9. **TRANSPORT.** Transport will move to the new area as soon as rations for tomorrow have been drawn. Cookers will proceed with the Transport.

10. **LEWIS GUN LIMBERS.** L.G. Limbers will report to Companies forthwith and will march in rear of Companies.

11. **BILLETS.** All billets must be left in a clean and sanitary condition and a certificate to this effect rendered to Orderly Room on arrival in the new area.

12. ACKNOWLEDGE.

(SGD) F.W.PALEY.
Capt. Adjutant,
20th Durham L.I.

29th June 1918.
Issued by runner at 2 p.m.
Copies to:-
No. 1 Filed.
No. 2 O.C. A Coy.
No. 3 O.C. B Coy.
No. 4 O.C. C Coy.
No. 5 O.C. D Coy.
Transport Officer - No. 6.
No. 7 Quartermaster.
No. 8 Medical Officer.
No. 9 R.S.M.

APPENDIX V.

SECRET. 20TH BN. DURHAM LIGHT INFANTRY Copy No......
ORDER NO. 76.

1. The Battalion will relieve "A" Battalion of the 102nd French Regt. tonight 30th inst., in the Right Sub-sector of the Divisional Front. The 217th Regt. of the 71st French Division will be on our right, and the 123rd Infantry Brigade on our left.
2. Time for the Battalion to move off will be notified later, together with detail concerning guides.
3. The Battalion will parade in fighting order with great-coats carried in bandolier fashion.
4. Lewis Gun Limbers will accompany Coys. as far forward as DE STER CABINET from which point Coys. will carry their Lewis Guns and S.A.A.
5. Owing to the Divisional relief extending over two days it is essential that as little movement as possible be made by daylight.
6. One French Officer per Coy. is remaining behind for 24 hours.
7. The Battalion will be under the command of the French G.O.C. until 3 a.m. July 2nd.
8. The S.O.S. Signal (3 White Stars) now used by the 7th French Division will remain in force until 3 a.m. 2nd July, after which the 2nd Army S.O.S. Signal (Red over Red over Red) will be used. S.O.S. Pistols and Cartridges (French) must be taken over tonight. These will be returned to Bn. H.Q. as soon as it is possible on the 2nd July.
9. No cooking is possible in the Forward Area. All cooking will, therefore, be done at the Transport Lines.
10. Telephones will be used very sparingly owing to the close proximity of the enemy. Runners will be used where possible. On no account will English be spoken over the telephone until after 3 a.m. July 2nd.
11. Water in the Forward Area is suspected of having been contaminated. and none, other than the supply sent up the line, will be used.
12. Packs will be plainly marked with the name and Coy. of the owner, and stacked at Coy. Billets by 7 p.m. The T.O. will arrange to collect them.
13. C Coy. will arrange to establish a Liaison Post, under an officer, at the Junction of the French with their right platoon.
14. All details left out of the line will parade at 8 p.m. outside the Transport Billet, under Lieut J.H.GARDNER.
15. The Transport Officer will arrange to mount one Anti-Aircraft Lewis Gun at "B" Echelon Transport Lines, which are being established at L.26.a.1.4. (Sheet 27).
16. Completion of relief will be reported to Battn. H.Q. by runner.
17. All copies of Air Photos, Defence Schemes and plans for Counter Attack will be taken over on relief.
18. ACKNOWLEDGE.

(SGD) F.W.PALEY.
Capt. Adjutant,
20th Bn. Durham Light Infantry.

30-6-18.
Issued by runner at 2.30 p.m.
Copies to:-

Copy No. 1	Filed	No. 6	Quartermaster.
No. 2	O.C. A Coy.	No. 7	Trabsport Officer.
No. 3	O.C. B COy.	No. 8	M.O.
No. 4	O.C. C Coy.	No. 9	R.S.M.
No. 5	O.C. D Coy.	No. 10	War Diary.

Army Form C. 2118.

WAR DIARY
INTELLIGENCE SUMMARY. 20th Bn. Durham. LIGHT. I
(Erase heading not required.)

Vol 27

Instructions regarding War Diaries and Intelligence Summaries are contained in F. S. Regs., Part II. and the Staff Manual respectively. Title pages will be prepared in manuscript.

Place	Date 1918 July	Hour	Summary of Events and Information	Remarks and references to Appendices
In trenches.	1st.		During the day the Battalion rested as much as possible. At night working parties and patrols were busy. Weather fine – observation good – stand-to lt	Het.
– do –	2nd.		Everyone rested as much as possible during the day. At night working parties and patrols were busy – Weather fine – observation good.	Het.
– do –	3rd.		Everyone rested as much as possible during the day – at night working parties were busy – Weather fine – observation good. Increased enemy artillery activity against our positions.	Het.
– do –	4th.		Everyone rested as much as possible during the day – at night working parties were busy – Weather fine – observation good.	Het.
– do –	5th.		Everyone rested as much as possible during the day – at night 5th & 6th, the Battalion were relieved by the 10th Battn. Queens R.W.Surrey Regt & move to Support relieving the 26th Battn. Royal Fusiliers.	Het. APPT
B# 14 F+5	6th.		Everyone rested as much as possible during the day. At night working parties were busy – Observation fair – weather fine. carrying parties	Het.

WAR DIARY
INTELLIGENCE SUMMARY

(Erase heading not required.)

Army Form C. 2118.

Instructions regarding War Diaries and Intelligence Summaries are contained in F.S. Regs., Part II. and the Staff Manual respectively. Title pages will be prepared in manuscript.

Place	Date 1918 JULY	Hour	Summary of Events and Information	Remarks and references to Appendices
In the trenches	7th		Everyone rested as much as possible during the day – Weather fine – observation good – At night working parties & carrying parties were busy	Hot.
– do –	8th		Everyone rested as much as possible during the day – Weather fine – observation good. – At night working parties & carrying parties were busy – Short thunderstorm about 10 p.m.	Hot.
– do –	9th		Everyone rested as much as possible during the day – Weather showery – Observation fair – At night working parties & carrying parties were busy.	Hot.
– do –	10th		Everyone rested as much as possible during the day – Weather fine – Observation good – The Battalion were relieved in support by the 10th Batt. Queens R.W. Surrey Regt on the night 10th/11th July. On completion of relief the Battalion took up billets in the Brigade Reserve area – Working parties were busy at night also	Hot. APP II
– do –	11th		During the day B Coy carried on work on building Brigade H.Q. Weather showery. Observation fair – A, C & D Coys worked during the night	Hot.

Army Form C. 2118.

WAR DIARY

INTELLIGENCE SUMMARY.

(Erase heading not required)

Instructions regarding War Diaries and Intelligence Summaries are contained in F. S. Regs., Part II. and the Staff Manual respectively. Title pages will be prepared in manuscript.

Place	Date	Hour	Summary of Events and Information	Remarks and references to Appendices
BILLETS.	12th		Weather showery. Observation fair - One boy worked during the day. Three boys at night - Baths at L.29.c.8.2 (BALLINGTON CAMP) were allotted to the Battalion.	See
— do —	13th		Weather fine - observation good - One company worked during the day - three companies at night.	See
— do —	14th		Weather showery - observation good - Working parties as for 13th. Advance parties proceeded to front line.	See
— do —	15th		Weather fine - observation fair - The Battalion relieved the 26th. Royal Fusiliers in the front line.	See APP III
— do —	16th		Weather generally fair during day - Thunderstorm at night - everyone rested as much as possible during the day - At night working parties were busy. Dispositions were altered according to Brigade Operation Orders.	See APP IV
— do —	17th		Weather fine with showers during the morning - observation good - everyone rested as much as possible during the day - Working parties were busy during the night.	See

WAR DIARY or INTELLIGENCE SUMMARY.

Army Form C. 2118.

(Erase heading not required.)

Place	Date 1918 June	Hour	Summary of Events and Information	Remarks and references to Appendices
In trenches	18th		Weather fine – observation good – Working parties were busy at night – everyone rested as much as possible during the day	–
– do –	19th		Weather fine – observation good – Everyone rested as much as possible during the day – Working parties were busy during the night	–
– do –	20th		Weather fine until 5pm to 9pm when showery – Everyone rested as much as possible during the day. The Battalion was relieved in front line by the 10th Battalion Queens Rt. Surrey Regt. & proceeded to support Battalion area.	APP V
– do –	21st		Working parties were busy during day & night. Everyone rested as much as possible – Weather fine. Observation good.	–
– do –	22nd		Weather showery – Working parties were busy both day and night.	–
– do –	23rd		Weather showery – Working parties were busy both day and night. Observation fair.	–
– do –	24th		Weather fine – Observation good – Working parties were busy both day and night.	–

WAR DIARY
INTELLIGENCE SUMMARY.
(Erase heading not required.)

Army Form C. 2118.

Instructions regarding War Diaries and Intelligence Summaries are contained in F. S. Regs., Part II. and the Staff Manual respectively. Title pages will be prepared in manuscript.

Place	Date 1918 July	Hour	Summary of Events and Information	Remarks and references to Appendices
In trenches	25th		Weather fine - observation good - Working parties were busy during the day - At night the Battalion were relieved by the 10th Bn. The Queens West Surrey Regiment and proceeded to area of Battalion in Brigade Reserve in the vicinity of Reninghelst	App VI
- do -	26th		Weather rainy - observation poor - Everyone rested as much as possible	App.
- do -	27th		Weather showery - observation fair - Working parties were busy during the day and night.	App.
- do -	28th		Weather fine - observation good - Working parties were busy during day + night	App.
- do -	29th		Weather fine - observation good - Working parties as usual.	App.
- do -	30th		Weather fine - observation fair - Working parties as usual.	App.
- do -	31st		Weather fine - observation good - Working parties as usual	App.

Commdg. 20th Durham L.I.

SECRET.   20th Bn. DURHAM LIGHT INFANTRY.   COPY NO....
                         ORDER NO. 77.
       ----

1.   The Battalion will be relieved on the night of the
5th/6th July, 1918 by the 10th Bn. "Queens" R.W.S. Regt.
        Each Company will be relieved by its opposite number.

2.   On relief, the Battalion will move into SUPPORT and
relieve the 26th Bn. Royal Fusiliers.

3.   All S.A.A., Bombs, Maps of the Line, Petrol Tins, S.O.S.
Grenades etc. will be handed over ob relief, and duplicate
receipts obtained and forwarded to this Office by 12 noon, 6th inst.

4.   An advance party from the "Queens" Regt. consisting of
Company Commanders, 1 N.C.O. per platoon and No. 1 of each
Lewis Gun Section, will arrive in the Line tonight.

5.   Each Company will detail one Officer to remain in the
Line, with the relieving unit, foe 24 hours.

6.   Companies will send their ration parties to draw rations
at IN DEN STER CABARET on arrival in the new positions.

7.   Arrival in the new positions will be reported to this Offfice
by runner, as sonn as relief of the 26th Bn. Royal Fusiliers has
been completed.

8.   Completion of relief in the front line psoitions will be
reported by wiring " YOUR G.10 RECEIVED ".
        Companies without a telephone will forward their report
by runner.

9.   Companies will carefully take over from Support Battalion
all S.A.A., Bombs etc., together with maps and plans for counter-
attack.

10.   All details concerning LIAISON with the Freanch will be
handed over to the "Queens" and taken over from the "Fusiliers".

11.   ACKNOWLEDGE.

                         (SGD) F.W. PALEY,
                                    Capt. & Adjutant,
4-7-1918.   20th Bn. Durham Light Infantry.

Issued by runner at 10.15 p.m.

Copy No. 1.   Filed.
Copy No. 2.   O.C. "A" Company.
Copy No. 3.   O.C. "B" Company.
Copy No. 4.   O.C. "C" Company.
Copy No. 5.   O.C. "D" Company.
Copy No. 6.   H.Q. Mess.
Copy No. 7.   Transport Officer.
Copy No. 8.   O.C. Details.
Copy No. 9.   O.C. Headquarters.

APP II

SECRET.   20TH BN. DURHAM LIGHT INFANTRY.   COPY NO.....
                ORDER NO. 78.

1.   The Battalion will be relieved in Support on the night of the 10/11th July, 1918 by the 10th Bn. "Queens" R.W.S. Regt. and after relief will move into the reserve area.

2.   All Defence Schemes, Plans of Work, A.A. Lewis Gun Positions, Petrol Tins, Trench Stores, S.O.S. Grenades etc. will be handed over to the relieving unit.
        Receipts in duplicate for Trench Stores etc. handed over will be forwarded to this office by 6.0 p.m. 11th July.

3.   Companies will be relievd by their oppposite numbers.

4.   1 Officer per Company, 1 Runner per Platoon of the "Queens" will join Companies tonight together with one runner per Company H.Qrs. One Officer and one N.C.O. will join Battn. Headquarters on the morning of the 10th inst.

5.   At 11.0 a.m. on the morning of the 10th inst. a party from this Battalion consisting of 1 N.C.O per Company, 1 runner per platoon and 1 from H.Q. will rendezvous at IN DEN STER CABARET (Ration Dump) and proceed to the new area at present occupied by the 26th Bn. Royal Fusiliers. The 4 runners per Company and the runner from H.Q. will re-join their Companies before 12 mid-night 10/11th inst.

6.   1 limber for H.Q. and the Lewis Gun limber of each Company will be at the IN DEN STER CABARET (Ration Dump) at 12.30 a.m on the 11th July. On no account will Lewis Guns be loaded before Companies are relieved.

7.   Rations will be delivered on arrival in the Reserve Area. C.Q.M.S's will arrange for cookers to be at Company billets and for a hot meal to be ready for Companies on arrival.

8.   The Transport Officer will arrange for Officers' Valises and Mess Kits to be delivered to Companies on night of 10/11th July.

9.   Completion of Relief in Support Lines will be notified by wiring "A.5 RECEIVED".

10. ACKNOWLEDGE.

                                (sgd) F.W. PALEY,

9-7-18.   Capt. & Adjutant.

Copy No. 1.   Filed.
Copy No. 2.   O.C. "A" Company.
Copy No. 3.   O.C. "B" Company.
Copy No. 4.   O.C. "C" Company.
Copy No. 5.   O.C. "D" Company.
Copy No. 6.   O.C. Headquarters.
Copy No. 7.   H.Q. Mess.
Copy No. 8.   Q.M. & T.O.

20TH BN. DURHAM LIGHT INFANTRY. ORDER NO. 22.

APP III

ADDENDUM.

In para 3. include 1 Subaltern from "A" & "C" Coys. 1 N.C.O. from H.Qrs.

Captain & Adjutant,
20th Bn. Durham Light Infantry.

SECRET.   20TH. BN. DURHAM LIGHT INFANTRY.   Copy No........
                              ORDER No. 72.
                        ----

1. On the night 15th/16th inst., the Battalion will relieve 26th
    Bn. Royal Fusiliers in the Front Line. The following will be
    the disposition of Coys.:-
    "B" Coy. Right Front Coy.   "D" Coy. Left Front Coy.
    "C" Coy. Support Coy.   "A" Coy. Reserve Coy.
2. All defence schemes, plans of work, details of working parties,
    trench maps, trench stores &c. will be taken over on relief.
    Copies of these will be forwarded to this Office immediately
    after dark on the night of the 16th inst.
3. Advance Parties as under will be sent forward tonight 14th inst:-
    Coy.Comdrs. of "B" & "D" Coys. 1 N.C.O. per platoon. 1 Signaller
    and 2 runners per Coy. No. 1 of each Lewis Gun Team. They
    will remain in the line until the Battalion relieves.
4. The Battalion will move off from Billets at 6-45 p.m. 15th inst.
    Intervals of 100 yards between Platoons and 200 yards between
    Companies will be maintained. The Battalion will move off in the
    following order - "B" "D" "C" & "A" "B.Hrs". Dress - Fighting
    Order and Great Coats carried in bandolier fashion
5. Guides from 26th Bn. Royal Fusiliers on the scale of 1 for
    Bn. H.Qrs. 1 for Coy. H.Qrs. and 1 per Platoon will wait for
    Battalion at DE SIGN CABINET.
6. 1 Limber for H.Qrs. and the Lewis Gun Limber for each Coy. will
    report at 6 p.m. 15th. Lewis Guns will be carried on Limbers
    as far as DE SIGN CABINET where they will be off loaded and
    carried into the line.
7. Coy.Comdrs. will ensure that each man fills his water bottle
    before moving into the line.
8. O.C. H.Qrs. will arrange for 2 bugles to be taken into the line.
9. 20 Magazines for each Lewis Gun will be taken into the line.
10. The Master Cook will arrange for tea to be sent up in petrol tins
    with each Coy. Lewis Gun Limber on night 15th inst.
11. An Advance Party from 10th Queens will report to Coys. on the
    morning of the 15th inst. Coys. will hand over details of work,
    trench stores, petrol tins and other details regarding this area.
    Receipts will be forwarded to this Office as early as possible.
12. All details left out of the line will parade at Battalion H.Qrs.
    at 6 p.m. under 2nd Lieuts. Russell & McDonald.
13. Officers valises, mess kits &c. will be stacked outside Coy.
    H.Qrs. by 5-30 p.m. 15th inst. The Transport Officer will
    arrange to collect these.
14. Completion of relief will be reported by wiring DOG to this
    Office.
15. Acknowledge.

                                           T W Paley
                                        Captain & Adjutant,
14.9.16th.   20th Bn. Durham Light Infantry.
Issued by runner at 10-45 p.m.
Copies to :-

Copy No. 1. Filed.   Copy No. 6. O.C.26th R.Fs.
  "   2. O.C. A Company.   "   7. Quartermaster.
  "   3. O.C. B Company.   "   8. Transport Officer.
  "   4. O.C. C Company.   "   9. Medical Officer.
  "   5. O.C. D Company.   "   10. R.S.M.
                                   "   11. War Diary.

SECRET.   20th Bn. DURHAM LIGHT INFANTRY.   COPY NO.....
ORDER NO. 80.

1. Re-Organisation of defence in accordance with 124th Infantry Brigade Defence Scheme, which was explained to all officers by the Commanding Officer whilst the Battalion was in RESERVE, will take place tonight 16/17th inst.

2. "B" Company will hold the front line in "Diamond" formation with 1 platoon in Support in the neighbourhood of FAIRY HOUSE

3. "A" Company accomodated in WEDGE WOOD BANK, with two platoons to man trenches about M.18.d.5.7. and 2 platoons trenches at M.18.b. along the line of MARJORIE LANE. These two latter platoons are to be available for immediate counter-attack.

4. B "D" Company will move to MARJORIE POST, with one platoon accomodated at about in the road at about M.17.d.75.75. This platoon will relieve a platoon of the support Battalion.

5. "C" Company will relieve the left front company in the line of resistance (this is the same position as last occupied by C Coy. when the Battalion was in Support).

6. It is most probable that the platoons of the support Battalion being relieved by platoons of this Battalion will be out on Working Parties when the relief takes place.

7. The change of dispositions of the front line will be effected as soon as possible after dark. "D" Company will move to their new positions immediately after being relieved by "B" Company.
    "C" Company will move to new position on receipt of message from O.C. "B" Company stating that the whole of "B" Coy. is in their new position.
    If, however, "B" Company's move is not complete by 1 a.m 17th inst., "C" Company will move without further delay.
    "A" Company will effect their move immediately after dark.

8. "B" Company will move the power buzzer and amplifier to their new Headquarters in the FAIRY HOUSE LINE.

9. "D" Company will move all ammunition, bombs etc with the exception of 1 box of S.A.A. which is to be left in each of the posts in the left "Diamond".(4 boxes in all).
    "C" Company will move all ammunition, bombs etc. with the exception of 3 boxes of S.A.A. to be left at Company Headquarters for the use of O.B. "B" Company.
    When in new positions O's.C. Companies will arrange to distribute all ammunition amongst their platoons.

10. Completion of Relief will be notified to this Office by runner.

11. ACKNOWLEDGE.

Capt. & Adjutant,
20th Bn. Durham Light Infantry.

16-7-18.

Issued by runner at 10 p.m.

Copy No. 1. Filed.
Copy No. 2. O.C. "A" Company.
Copy No. 3. O.C. "B" Company.
Copy No. 4. O.C. "C" Company.
Copy No. 5. O.C. "D" Company.
Copy No. 6. O.C. 26th Royal Fusiliers.

SECRET.　　　　　　1ST AMENDMENT TO ORDER NO.80.　　　　　SECRET.

Delete para.7 and substitute the follwoing :-

　　　　The change of dispositions in Frnt Line will be effected as soon as possible after dark.
　　　　As the platoons of "D" Company are relieved they will commence wiring on the new Front Line positions (the wiring of the"DIAMONDS"). They will cease work at 2 a.m. and then move to their new positions. A small a party as possible should be detailed to carry rations to new positions.
　　　　"C" Company will not wait to be relieved, but will move immediately after dark to "MARJORIE POST" where they will be employed on digging unti about 2.0 a.m. This Company should carry S.A.A., Bombs etc. to scene of work.
After work is finished they should be carried to new psoitions.
　　　　"A" Company will efffect their move immediately after dark, and will then proceed for work on MARJORIE POST.

ACKNOWLEDGE.

16-7-18.　　　　　　　　　　　　　　　　Capt. & Adjutant,
　　　　　　　　　　　　　　　　　20th Bn. Durham Light Infantry.

Issued to all, recipients of Order No. 80.

APP V

SECRET.   20TH BN. DURHAM LIGHT INFANTRY.   COPY NO.....
               ORDER NO. 81.
               ----

1.   On the night of the 20/21st July, 1918, the Battalion will be relieved in the front line by the 10th Bn. "Queens" R.W.S. Regiment.

2.   Companies of the "Queens" relieving Companies of this Battalion will be notified by advance parties from the "Queens".

3.   All Defence Schemes, Plans of Work, Trench Stores, Details Of Working Parties, Maps etc. will be handed over on relief and receipts in duplicate forwarded to this office by 10.30 p.m. 21st inst.

4.   Instructions with regard to Working Parties will be issued later.

5.   The usual advance parties from the 10th "Queens" will report to Companies tonight.

6.   Companies will send 1 N.C.O. and 1 runner per platoon and 1 Officer and 1 runner per Company to report to Headquarters 26th Royal Fusiliers early on the morning of the 20th inst. This party will be directed to Companies they are to relieve by 26th Royal Fusiliers. "B" Company's Party will report to these Headquarters (CLIFF) just before dawn on the morning of the 20th inst. 2/Lieut. BASSETT will proceed to the new area for "B" Company.

7.   Guides on a scale of 1 per Company H.Q., and 1 for each platoon will meet relieving unit at IN DEN STER CABARET at 10.30 p.m. 1 guide for Battalion H.Q. will also be provided.

8.   On relief the Battalion will move into Support and will relieve the 26th Bn. Royal Fusiliers as follows:-

A Company 20th D.L.I. will relieve B Company 26th Royal Fusiliers.
B Company   -do-   -do- A Company   -do-
C Company   -do-   -do- C Company   -do-
D Company   -do-   -do- D Company   -do-

9.   Runners sent in advance to 26th Bn. Royal Fusiliers will return to Companies as soon as it is dark on the night of 20/21st inst. to guide platoons to new positions.

10.   Rations on night of relief will be dumped at DEN STER CABARET at 1 a.m. 21st inst.
        Companies will arrange to collect rations as soon as possible after relief. C.Q.M.S's will remain with rations until this is done.

11.   Completion of Relief by 10th "Queens" will be reported by wiring "BIRD".
        Relief of 26th Bn. Royal Fusiliers will be reported by wiring "GOT IT".

12.   ACKNOWLEDGE.

                              (Sgd) F. W. PALEY,
                                     Capt. & Adjutant,
19-7-18.   20th Bn. Durham Light Infantry.

Issued to Signals at 10 p.m.

APP VI

SECRET.   20TH BN. DURHAM LIGHT INFANTRY.   COPY NO...
                    ORDER NO. 82.
            ----

1. (a)   On the night of the 25/26th July, 1918, the Battalion will be relieved in Support by the 10th Bn. "Queens" R.W.S. Regt.
   (b)   On relief the Battalion will move into reserve in the RENINGHELST AREA.

2.   Companies will be relieved by their opposite numbers of the 10th Bn. "Queens" R.W.S. Regt.

3.   All Defence Schemes, A.A. Lewis Gun Positions, Plans of work, Trench Stores, Maps etc. will be handed over on relief and duplicate receipts obtained and forwarded to this office by 6 p.m 26th inst.

4.   An advance party from the 10th Bn. "Queens" Regt. will report to Companies on the morning of the 25th inst.

5.   Instructions regarding Working Parties for night of relief will be issued later.
     Companies on working parties will carry with them 4 Lewis Guns and 10 Magazines per Gun. Remaining guns and magazines will be sent to new area on Lewis Gun Limbers.

6.   1 limber for Battalion H.Q. and 1 Limber per Company will report to Company ration dumps at 12 mid-night on night of relief.

7.   An advance party consisting as under will proceed to H.Q. 26th Royal Fusiliers at BRASSERIE - RENINGHELST on the morning of the 25th inst:-
        1 Officer, 1 N.C.O. and 2 runners from Headquarters.
        1 Officer, 1 N.C.O. and 1 runner per Company H.Qrs.
        1 runner per platoon.

All runners will return to Companies not later than 7 p.m. 25th inst. and will act as guides for platoons.

8.   Companies will takeover from opposite numbers of the 26th Royal Fusiliers in the Reserve Area.

9.   Rations will be delivered to Company Ration Dumps in Reserve Area on night of 25th inst. C.Q.M.S's will remain with rations until Companies can collect them.
     Advance officers will ascertain from 26th Royal Fusiliers the position of Company Ration Dumps.

10. Cooking arrangements for Reserve Area will be notified later.

11. Completion of relief in Support will be notified by wiring
333. Companies will also report arrival in billets in RENINGHELST.

12. Officers' valises will be delivered to Companies, if possible, on night of relief.

13.   ACKNOWLEDGE.

                              (SGD) F.W. PALEY,
                                   Capt. Adjutant,
                              20th Bn. Durham Light Infantry.
24-7-1918.

Issued to sigals at 10 p.m.

Copy No. 1. Filed.   Copy No. 6   O.C. Headquarters.
Copy No. 2. O.C. A Company.   Copy No. 7. Q.M. & T.O.
Copy No. 3. O.C. B Company.   Copy No. 8. O.C. 10th "Queens"
Copy No. 4. O.C. C Company.   Copy No. 9. O.C. 26th R. F's.
Copy No. 5. O.C. D Company.

Army Form C. 2118.

WAR DIARY
INTELLIGENCE SUMMARY.
(Erase heading not required.)

Instructions regarding War Diaries and Intelligence Summaries are contained in F. S. Regs., Part II. and the Staff Manual respectively. Title pages will be prepared in manuscript.

Place	Date	Hour	Summary of Events and Information	Remarks and references to Appendices
IN TRENCHES	1918 Aug. 1st		Weather fine – observation fair – Working parties were busy during the day and night.	Apt.
— do —	2nd		Weather sunny – observation fair – The Battalion was organised in two companies. Battalions together with the 1st Battalion, 108th Infantry Regiment (U.S.) & moved from Reserve area to front line & support. "A" & B coys (British) & A&B coys (American) formed one Battalion, took over front line system known as "A". The 106th Infantry Regiment (U.S.). "C" & "D" coys (British) & C & D coys (American) formed Support Battalion Known as "B" and relieved the 26th Battalion, Royal Fusiliers in Support line system. Casualties:- 2nd Lieut. S. Kent accidentally injured by collapse of dugout.	APP I
— do —	3rd.		Weather fine – observation good – Everyone rested as much as possible during the day – at night working parties were busy	Ht-
— do —	4th		Weather showery- observation fair – Working parties were detailed to day & night work Lieut. Thos Riley was wounded and at duty.	Ht-
— do —	5th		Weather fine during the day & showery in the evening – observation good – "A" Battalion was relieved by "B" Battalion in front line system & moved	Ht- APP II

WAR DIARY
INTELLIGENCE SUMMARY
(Erase heading not required.)

Army Form C. 2118.

Place	Date 1918 Aug.	Hour	Summary of Events and Information	Remarks and references to Appendices
IN TRENCHES	5.		To Support line system - Relief complete by 1.40 am. Casualties - Nil	App
-do-	6.		Weather showery in morning - fine in afternoon. - Observation good - Working parties were busy day and night. Casualties Nil	App
-do-	7.		Weather fine - observation good - the 1st Battalion. 108th Infantry Regiment took over the front line system from B. company. Battalion - Bombardt. Battalion were distanced + 20 of Battalion, the Durham L.I. took over. Support line system. Relief complete 1.40 am. Casualties - 1 O.R.	App
-do-	8.		Weather fine - observation good - working parties were busy most by day. Casualties nil. A raiding party of the 108th Bavr. Greens. Royal West Surrey Regiment. a penetration of our enemy lines and inflicted casualties on the enemy. captured 1 prisoner + 1 trophy	App
-do-	9.		Further low visibility good - working parties were busy during the day. Casualties Nil	App
-do-	10		The Battalion were relieved by D Company Battalion composed of 11th D.R.L. East. Regt. and part of 108th Infantry Regt. (U.S.) 3rd Battalion	App

Army Form C. 2118.

WAR DIARY
or
INTELLIGENCE SUMMARY.
(Erase heading not required.)

Place	Date	Hour	Summary of Events and Information	Remarks and references to Appendices
In trenches	10		and moved into the vicinity of REMINGHELST (Reserve Battalion area) Relief completed by 2am Casualties = NIL	Ats
– do –	11		Weather fine – visibility good – 1 Company worked on Brigade H.Q. + three companies rested. Casualties = NIL	Ats
– do –	12		Weather fine – visibility good – 1 Company worked on Brigade H.Q. + 3 Companies carried out inspections and interior economy.	Ats
– do –	13		Weather fine – visibility good – 1 Company worked on Brigade H.Q and the remainder carried out training as far as possible – Casualties = NIL	Ats
– do –	14		Weather fine – visibility good – 1 Company worked on Brigade H.Q and two Companies on the Scherpenberg and Dickebusch Lake Line – 1 Company rested. Casualties – four.	Ats
– do –	15		Weather fine – visibility good – 1 Company worked on Brigade H.Q + one on the SCHERPENBERG – DICKEBUSCH LAKE LINE – two companies carried out training. Casualties NIL	Ats

Army Form C. 2118.

WAR DIARY
or
INTELLIGENCE SUMMARY.
(Erase heading not required.)

Instructions regarding War Diaries and Intelligence Summaries are contained in F. S. Regs., Part II. and the Staff Manual respectively. Title pages will be prepared in manuscript.

Place	Date 1918 Aug	Hour	Summary of Events and Information	Remarks and references to Appendices
IN TRENCHES	16		Weather fine – visibility good – Work – 1 company on Brigade Hq. during the day – two companies on SCHERPENBERG – DICKEBUSCH LAKE LINE at night – One company carried out training and range practice on 30+ range – Casualties – NIL	Nil
– do –	17		Weather fine – visibility good until 5.30 p.m. showery until 8.30 p.m. – Visibility fair – Work – 1 company worked on Brigade Hq. – Two companies on the SCHERPEN- BERG – DICKEBUSCH LAKE LINE at night – 1 Company carried out training and range practice on 30+ range – Casualties – NIL	Nil
– do –	18		Weather fine – visibility fair – Work – 1 company Brigade Hq.(day) two companies SCHERPENBERG – DICKEBUSCH LAKE LINE at night – one company rested – Casualties – NIL	Nil
– do –	19		Weather fine – visibility good – Work – 2 company Brigade Hq. on the SCHERPENBERG – DICKEBUSCH LAKE LINE at night. Two companies carried out training during the day – Casualties – 2 killed + 2 wounded	Nil

WAR DIARY
INTELLIGENCE SUMMARY.
(Erase heading not required.)

Army Form C. 2118.

Place	Date 1918 Aug.	Hour	Summary of Events and Information	Remarks and references to Appendices
IN TRENCHES	20		Weather fine - visibility good - Companies carried out training during the day. - Battalion working party and cancelled - Casualties - NIL	Apt
- do -	21		Weather fine - visibility good - Companies carried out training during the day. Two companies worked at night on Bokenberg - Richebed Lake line - Casualties - NIL	Apt
- do -	22		Weather fine - visibility good - Companies carried out training during the day. Two companies worked at night on Bokenberg - Dickebusch Lake Line. - Casualties - NIL	
- do -	23		Weather fine during day - slight rain at night - The Battalion relieved the 26th Battalion Royal Fusiliers in the front line - Relief complete by 11.35 p.m. - "C" company worked on the Bokenberg - Dickebusch Lake Line at night - Casualties - NIL	APP IV
- do -	24		Weather fine - Observation of L. Europe rates so much as to avoid clearing the day - Working parties were busy at night - Casualties - No Casualties	Apt

Army Form C. 2118.

WAR DIARY
or
INTELLIGENCE SUMMARY.
(Erase heading not required.)

Place	Date 1918 Aug.	Hour	Summary of Events and Information	Remarks and references to Appendices
IN TRENCHES.	25.		Weather fine during day – heavy rain fell at 9 pm continued showery all night. Visibility fair – Everyone rested as much as possible during the day – Working parties were busy at night – Casualties – NIL	thus
– do –	26		Weather showery. Visibility poor – Everyone rested as much as possible during the day – Working parties were busy at night – Casualties – Three missing	thus
– do –	27		Weather fair – visibility fair – Everyone rested as much as possible during the day – Working parties were busy at night – Casualties – NIL	thus
– do –	28		Weather showery – visibility fair – Everyone rested as much as possible during the day – Working parties were busy at night. Casualties – One OR died – 1 OR died of wounds	thus
– do –	29		Weather fair – visibility fair – Everyone rested as much as possible during the day – At 9 p.m. 10/2 Bn Queens R.W. Surrey Regt relieved the Battalion in the front line, the Batt. then moved into Lytton –	thus APP V

Army Form C. 2118.

WAR DIARY
or
INTELLIGENCE SUMMARY.
(Erase heading not required.)

Instructions regarding War Diaries and Intelligence Summaries are contained in F.S. Regs., Part II. and the Staff Manual respectively. Title pages will be prepared in manuscript.

Place	Date 1918 Aug	Hour	Summary of Events and Information	Remarks and references to Appendices
IN TRENCHES	30.		Weather fine - chilly - Visibility - poor - The enemy withdrew from the outer onslaught in front of us. - Strong patrols were pushed out to gain contact - Casualties: - NIL	
–do–	31.		Weather fine - Visibility good - Casualties. NIL. Battalion remained in Divisional Reserve	

Commanding Officer
(Signature)
1st Bn.

SECRET.   20TH BN. DURHAM LIGHT INFANTRY.   COPY NO...
                    ORDER NO. 83.
           ----

1. (a) On the night of the 2nd/3rd August 1918, "A" Battalion -
20th Bn. Durham Light Infantry & Americans - will relieve 1st Battn.
106th Regiment, 27th American Division in the Frnt Line.
   (b) "B" Battalion - 20th Bn. Durham Light Infantry & Americans -
will relieve 26th Bn. Royal Fusiliers in Support the same evening.
2.   No. 1. Company "A" Battalion will relieve "A" Company
106th Regiment (American).
        No. 2. Company "A" Battalion will relieve "B" Company,
106th Regiment (American).
        No. 3. Company "A" Battalion will relieve "C" Company,
106th Regiment (American).
        No. 4. Company "A" Battalion will relieve "D" Company,
106th Regiment (American).
3.   No. 1. Company "B" Battalion will relieve "A" Company,
26th Bn. Royal Fusiliers.
        No. 2. Company "B" Battalion will relieve "C" Company,
26th Bn. Royal Fusiliers.
        No. 3. Company "B" Battalion will relieve "B" Company
26th Bn. Royal Fusiliers.
        No. 4. Company "B" Battalion will relieve "D" Company
26th Bn. Royal Fusiliers.
4. (a) 1 Guide for Coy. Headquarters and 1 for each Platoon from the
106th Regiment (American) will meet Companies of "A" Battalion
at IN DEN STER CABARET at 10.30 p.m.
   (b) The same nomber of guides as above from the 26th Bn. R.F's
will meet Companies of "B" Battalion at IN DEN STER CABARET at 11.15 p.m.
5.   1 Limber for Headquarters and 1 for each Company will report
to Companies about 9.15 p.m. on the evening of the 2nd/3rd August.
All Lewis Guns, Trench Bundles etc. will be off-loaded at IN DEN STER
CABARET and carried into the line.
6.   1 Lewis Gun Limber per American Company, each containing 8
Lewis Guns, Officers' Trench Bundles, Mess Kits etc. will join
Companie about 9 p.m. on nightof 2nd/3rd August. Companies will
arrange for a reliable guide to meet these limbers and conduct them
to the present area of Companies.   These limbers will then proceed
up the line in rear of Companies and will off-load at IN DEN STER
CABARET.   Guides will meet limbers at Cross Roads 28/0.32.d.7.3.
7.   Companies will take over all Defence Schemes, Plans of
Work, S.O.S. Grenades, Trench Stores etc. and will forward
duplicate receipts to "A" & "B" Battalion H.Q. respectively as soon
as possible after relief.
8.   Rations for the night 2nd/3rd August will be delivered to
Companies about 9.15 p.m. and will be carried into the Line on the man.
A certain amount of tea is being arranged for, and this can be taken
forward on Lewis Gun Limbers.
9. (a) "A" Battalion will move off first in the following order:-
No. 3, No. 4, No. 2, No. 1 Companies and H.Q.
        The leading Company will pass the StartingPoint - Fork Roads
at M.5.a.15.30 at 10 p.m.   Companies will maintain 10 yards interval
between Platoons and 200 yards between Companies.
   (b) "B" Battalion will move off in the following order:-
        No. 1, No. 2, No. 3, No. 4 Companies and H.Q.
        The leading Company will pass the starting point as for
"A" Battalion at 10.45 p.m.   The same distances between Platoons
and Companies will be maintained as for "A" Battalion.
10.   Companies will hand over in this Area all Defence Schemes,
S.O.S. Grenades, Trench Stores, including harvestinf sickles etc.
to advance parties of the 26th Bn. Royal Fusiliers. Duplicate receipts
for these stores will be forwarded to Bn. H.Q. by 6 p.m. 2nd August.
11.   Completion of Relief by "A" & "B" Battalions will be reported
by wiring initials of Company Commander and the time, to the
respectively Battalion H.Q.
12.   ACKNOWLEDGE.

                        (SGD) F.W. PALEY
                                Capt. & Adjutant,
28-18.   20th Bn. Durham Light Infantry.

SECRET.   20TH BN. DURHAM LIGHT INFANTRY.   COPY NO....
                                    ORDER NO. 84.
                          ----

1. (a) On the night of the 5th/6th August, the Battalion will relieve "A" Battalion in the Front Line.
   (b) Companies will take over the Line as follows:-

No. 1. Company "B" Battalion will relieve No. 4 Company "A" Battalion.
No. 2. Company   -do-   No. 3. Company   -do-
No. 3. Company   -do-   No. 1 Company   -do-
No. 4. Company   -do-   No. 2 Company   -do-

2. Guides on a scale of 1 per Company H.Q. and 1 for each Platoon will report to Companies from "A" Battalion in the afternoon.

3. Dispositions of "A" Battalion in the Front Line are as follows:-
   No. 3. Company - Front Line.
   No. 4. Company - WEDGEWOOD BANK.
   No. 2. Company - MARJORIE POST.
   No. 1. Company - N. of SCHERPENBERG.

4. All Companies, excepting Company moving to Front Line, will send one N.C.O. to take over stores in daylight.

5. Companies will move off in the following order as soon as light permits:- No. 2, No. 1, No. 3 & No. 4 Companies. Care will be taken to avoid Companies crowding up close to one another.

6. ALL details of work, S.O.S., Trench Stores defence schemes etc. will be handed over on relief. Duplicate receipts will be forwarded to this Office as soon as possible after relief.

7. One N.C.O. from "A" Battalion will report to Companies on the 5th inst. to take over. All stores details of work, defence schemes, etc. will be handed over to him and duplicate receipts forwarded to this office by 8 p.m. 5th inst.

8. Rations for night of the 5th/6th inst. will be brought up on mules and Companies will send guides to meet mules at 12 m.n. at these Headquarters. The Company moving to the Front Line need not send guides as one will be provided by Battalion H.Q.
   These guides will conduct guides to the following places where rations will be off-loaded:-
No. 1 & No. 4 Companies - to Old Bn. H.Q. in Front Line (near MARJORIE POST
No. 2. Company   - to Front Line Coy. H.Q.
No. 3. Company   - to Junction of DEN STER CABARET Track with
                          LOCRE - LA CLYTTE Road.
   Companies will arrange to collect rations from these dumps as soon as possible.

9. All empty petrol tins will be dumped at the present ration dumps of Companies before Companies move off. The Transport Officer will arrange to collect these tins.

10. Both "A" & "B" Battalion H.Qrs. will remain where they are at present situated.

11. Completion of relief will be notified by wiring "BROWN" and the time.

12. ACKNOWLEDGE.

                                        (SGD) F. WELFORD.

5-9-18.   2/Lieut. Adjt.,
                                                 "B" Battalion.

SECRET.

Copy.

APP II

20TH BN. DURHAM LIGHT INFANTRY.
ORDER NO. 86.

COPY NO...

1. On the night of the 10th/11th inst. the Battalion will be relieved by "D" Composite Battalion of the 10th Bn. "Queens" R.W.S. Regt. and Americans.

2. Companies will be relieved as under :-

   No. 1. Company "D" Composite Bn. relieves "D" Company D.L.I.
   No. 2.   -do-   "A"   -do-
   No. 3.   -do-   "C"   -do-
   No. 4.   -do-   "B"   -do-

3. The usual Guides one per Company H.Q. and one for each platoon will meet the relieving unit at IN DEN STER CABARET at 11 p.m.

4. All Defence Schemes and Plans of Work, Trench Stores, Trench Maps etc. will be handed over on relief. A Copy of receipts for above stores will be forwarded to reach this office by noon 11th inst.

5. Each Company will detail one Officer and one Senior N.C.O. (Sgt. or Cpl.) per Company and 1 junior N.C.O. per Platoon to remain behind with the relieving unit. Rations for the 11th inst for these parties will be sent up on night of the 10/11th inst. on Company Lewis Gun Limbers. Rations for succeeding days will be handed over by the Q.M. to the Q.M. 10th Bn. "Queens" R.W.S. Regt. for delivery. These Officers and N.C.O's will re-join the Battalion on the night of the 16th/17th inst.

6. 1 Limber for H.Q. and the Lewis Gun Limbers of each Company will report to Companies ration dumps at 12 m.n. on night of 10th/11th inst.

7. (a) On relief the Battalion will move to Reserve in the RENINGHELST AREA. Companies will relieve opposite numbers of the 26th Bn. Royal Fusiliers.
   (b) Each Company will send an advance party of 1 Officer, 1 N.C.O. and 4 runners to report to the H.Qrs. of the 26th Bn. Royal Fusiliers not later than 3 p.m. on the 10th inst. The 4 runners will return to their Companies before 8 p.m. and will then act as guides to the New Positions.

8. The Q.M. will arrange for Tailors, Shoemakers etc. to proceed to RENINGHELST on night of relief. Officers' Valises and Mess Kits will be delivered to Companies in New Area on night of the 10/11th inst.

9. Rations for the night of relief will be delivered to Company Dumps in the New Area. Companies will arrange for the N.C.O. taking over from the 26th Royal Fusiliers to meet rations at the Company Dumps.

10. (a). Completion of relief by "D" Composite Battalion will be reported by wiring Company Commanders initials and the time.
    (b) Companies will alos report when they are established in the new positions.

11. Companies will ensure that their Area is left clean.

12. ACKNOWLEDGE.

(SGD) F.W. PALEY,
Capt. & Adjutant,
20th Bn. Durham Light Infantry.

9-8-18.

Copy.   APP. IV

SECRET.   20TH BN DURHAM LIGHT INFANTRY.   COPY NO:..
                         ORDER NO. 87.
                 ----

1.   On the night of the 23rd/24th August 1918 the 20th Bn. Durham L.I.
will relieve the 26th Bn. Royal Fusiliers in the Front Line.

2.   C Coy. 20th D.L.I. will relieve B Coy. R.F's in Front Line.
     B Coy. 20th D.L.I. will relieve C Coy. 26th R.F's in WEDGEWOOD BANK.
     D Coy. 20th D.L.I. will relieve D Coy. 26th R.F's at MARJORIE POST.
     A Coy. 20th D.L.I. will relieve A Coy. 26th R.F's in Reserve -
                                                      N. of SCHERPENBERG.

3.   1 Guide for Company Headquarters and 1 for each Platoon from the
26th Bn. Royal Fusiliers will meet Companies at House at M.17.a.45.90.
at 10.30 p.m.

4.   Rations for night 23rd/24th August will be delivered to Companies
about 9.45 p.m. and will be carried on the man into the line. Ration
Limbers will be loaded with Lewis Guns, Trench Bundles etc. and will
proceed in rear of Companies. They will be off-loaded at
M.17.a.46.90.   Limber for H.Q. will be off-loaded at Support Bn. H.Q.

5.   Companies will take over all Defence Schemes, Plans of Work,
S.O.S. Grenades, Trench Stores etc. and will forward duplicate receipts
to Bn. H.Q. as soon as possible after relief.

6.   The following routes will be taken by Companies - in order -
C, D & B:-
Track running from M.4.d.50.25. to M.4.a.15.40 -along RENINGHELST
CANADA CORNER Road to M.17.a.45.90. Thence by PIONEER C.T. forward.
Leading Company to pass M.6.d.50.25 at 10.10 p.m. "A" Company will
move at 10.20 p.m. via MORK ROAD at M.5.a.15.30. along RENINGHELST -
CANADA CORNER ROAD to M.17.a.45.90. Thence by PIONEER C.T. forward
Companies will maintain 100 yards interval between platoons and
200 yards between Companies.

7.   Companies will hand over in this Area all Defence Schemes, S.O.S.
Grenades, Trench Stores, including harvesting sickles, scythes etc.
to Advance Parties of the 10th Bn. "Queens" R.W.S. Regt. Duplicate
receipts for these stores will be forwarded to Bn. H.Q. by 6 p.m. 23rd.

8.   Officers' Kits, Mess Kits etc. for return to Transport
Lines will be stacked at Coy. Ration Dumps at 9 p.m. O's.C. Companies
will each detail 2 men who will be proceeding to the Brigade
Reinforcement Company to act as guard over htese dumps. The
Quartermaster will arrange to collect these kits etc.

9.   Completion of relief will xxxxxxxxx be reported by wiring
"COSY" and the Time to Battalion H.Q.

                                    (SGD) F.W. PALEY,
                                          Capt. & Adjutant,
23-8-18.   20th Bn. Durham Light Infantry.

Issued to Signals at 9.0 a.m.

Copy No. 1. Filed.   Copy No. 6 O.C. Headquarters.
Copy No. 2. O.C. "A" Company.   Copy No. 7. Quartermaster.
Copy No. 3. O.C. B Company.   Copy No. 8. O.C. 26th Bn. R.F's.
Copy No. 4. O.C. "C" Company.   Copy No. 9. H.Q. Mess.
Copy No. 5. O.C. "D" Company.   Copy No. 10 War Diary.

SECRET   20th Bn. DURHAM L.I.   COPY NO.

APP. V

ORDER NO. 89.

1. The Battalion will be relieved in the Front Line on night of 29th/30th August, 1918 by the 10th Bn "Queens" R.W.S. Regt.

2. Coys will be relieved as under:—

"B" Coy 20th D.L.I. will be relieved by "B" Coy 10th Queens
"C" Coy   — do —   "C" Coy — do —
"D" Coy   — do —   "A" Coy — do —
"A" Coy   — do —   "D" Coy — do —

3. On being relieved the Battn will move into Support, taking over the area vacated by 10th Bn "Queens" R.W.S. Regt.

Coys will take over areas vacated by their opposite numbers.

4. An advance party consisting of 1 Officer and 1 runner per Coy, 1 N.C.O. & 1 Runner per platoon will report to O.C. 10th Bn "Queens" R.W.S. Regt early on the morning of the 29th inst, and will take over all Defence Schemes, Maps, Plans of Work, Trench Stores etc.

The 1 runner per Coy and the 1 N.C.O. per platoon will rejoin their Coys on the night of 29th August and will act as guides to the new positions.

5. The Quartermaster will arrange for rations for 30th inst to be dumped at the following places at 12 M.N. 29th/30th August.

"A" Coy — DEN STER CABARET
"B" Coy —   — do —
"D" Coy — Vicinity of Bn HQ
"C" Coy — SCHERPENBERG
HQ   —   — do —

- 2 -

O.C. Coys will arrange to collect rations as early as possible.

C.Q.M.S. will remain with rations until arrival of ration parties.

6. O.C. Coys will ensure that all petrol Tins, not Trench Stores, are carried to the new positions in SUPPORT and handed over to Transport on night 29/30 Aug. for return to Quartermaster.

7. Duplicate receipts for Trench Stores etc. handed over in the Front Line and taken over in Support will be forwarded to Battn. H.Q. by 6 p.m. 30th August.

8. Completion of Relief in the Front Line will be reported by wiring "YOUR G100 RECEIVED" followed by time.

Coys will report arrival in new positions by wiring name of Coy Commander + time.

9. Instructions regarding Working Parties for night of 29/30th inst. will be issued later.

10. ACKNOWLEDGE

A. Littlefield
Lieut Asst Adjt
20th Bn Durham L.I.

29-8-18
Issued to Signals at 9.0 p.m.
Copy No 1 — Filed
     No 2 — O.C. A Coy
     No 3 — O.C. B Coy
     No 4 — O.C. C Coy
     No 5 — O.C. D Coy
     No 6 — O.C. H.Q.
     No 7 — Quartermaster
     No 8 — O.C. ¾ Bn Queens R. of S. Regt
     No 9 — War Diary

Army Form C. 2118.

4 September 1918

WAR DIARY
or
INTELLIGENCE SUMMARY

20th Bn. Durham L.I.

WO 29

Place	Date	Hour	Summary of Events and Information	Remarks and references to Appendices
IN TRENCHES	1.		Weather fine - visibility good - At night the Battalion were relieved in front line by the 10th/11th Battalion Wiltshire Regiment, and moved to Reserve area at about 28.d.9.36 - Casualties - NIL	See App. I
– do – & Billets	2.		Weather fine - visibility good - Everyone rested as much as possible during the day - At night the Battalion relieved the 1st Battalion 105th American Infantry Regiment in front line in the DICKEBUSCH AREA. Relief complete 3.40 a.m. Casualties:- LIEUT. G.H. TOMPSON - 2 N.C.O's wounded.	
IN TRENCHES	3.		Weather fair - visibility fair - Front line organised as much as possible. Casualties. NIL	do.
– do –	4.		Weather fine until night when slight showers occurred - visibility good - Battalion attacked enemy Artillery - Some objectives taken but Battalion unable on account of flares hung up heavily to hold fresh ground. Casualties - Officers - KILLED - 2ND LT E. RUSSELL + 2ND LT J.S. WILLIS 2ND LT. W. EPPSTEIN (N.N.D-GAS- LT COL. A.V.R. GAYER (C.S.O Wounded) + 2ND LT P.T. CONRATH - Wounded:- 2ND. LT T.H. BASSETT, 2ND LT C.G. LAVELL, 2ND LT A. MACLAREN, LT F. BRUNT. 25 Other Ranks - Killed	do.

WAR DIARY
INTELLIGENCE SUMMARY
(Erase heading not required)

Army Form C. 2118.

Instructions regarding War Diaries and Intelligence Summaries are contained in F.S. Regs., Part II. and the Staff Manual respectively. Title pages will be prepared in manuscript.

Place	Date 1918 SEPT.	Hour	Summary of Events and Information	Remarks and references to Appendices
In Trenches	4 (cont)		The Battalion were relieved in the line by the 26th Battn. Royal Fusiliers and proceeded to Reninghelst near DICKEBUSCH.	A+
-do- & Billets	5		Weather fine - visibility good - Everyone rested as much as possible during the day. Casualties - NIL. The Battalion moved to Siffret Brigade area on Sheet 28 G. 36.	A+
-do- Billets	6		Weather fine - visibility good - Preparation of platoons & general cleaning of arms & equipment was carried out. Casualties - NIL	A+
-do-	7		Weather fair - heavy thunderstorms during afternoon - company training carried out. Casualties - NIL	A+
-do-	8		Weather showery - visibility fair - companies carried out rifle practices on ranges. Casualties - NIL	A+
-do-	9		Weather showery - visibility fair - companies carried out training in vicinity of billets. Casualties - NIL	A+

WAR DIARY
INTELLIGENCE SUMMARY.
(Erase heading not required.)

Army Form C. 2118.

Instructions regarding War Diaries and Intelligence Summaries are contained in F. S. Regs., Part II. and the Staff Manual respectively. Title pages will be prepared in manuscript.

Place	Date 1918 SEPT	Hour	Summary of Events and Information	Remarks and references to Appendices
BILLETS & TRENCHES	10		Weather showery and windy - visibility fair - Companies carried out training in vicinity of billets - Casualties - NIL.	Att
- do -	11		Weather showery and windy - visibility fair - One company worked during the day and three at night. - Casualties - three killed, 9 ORs wounded.	Att
- do -	12		Weather showery and windy - visibility fair - One company worked during the day and three at night - Casualties - NIL	Att
- do -	13		Weather fine - visibility good - One company worked during the day - and three at night - Casualties - NIL	Att
- do -	14		Weather showery - visibility fair - One company worked during the day - At night the Battalion moved to the Siffenhock Area on being relieved in support Brigade area by the 23rd. Battalion, Middlesex Regiment - Casualties - NIL	Att
IN BILLETS	15		Weather fine - The Battalion entrained at Siffenhock siding at 6am. and moved by trench gauge railway to LUMBRES thence by motor garage to BONNINGUES where the Battalion were billetted in the Reserve Brigade training area. - Casualties - NIL Transport moved by march route.	Att

WAR DIARY
INTELLIGENCE SUMMARY.
(Erase heading not required.)

Army Form C. 2118.

Instructions regarding War Diaries and Intelligence Summaries are contained in F. S. Regs., Part II. and the Staff Manual respectively. Title pages will be prepared in manuscript.

Place	Date	Hour	Summary of Events and Information	Remarks and references to Appendices
In Billets	16.		Weather fine – visibility good – Companies carried out training on the training area. "B" coy. fired musketry practices on range at AUDREHEM. Three companies carried out internal economy and drill	AJJ
– do –	17		Weather fine – visibility good – Three companies carried out tactical training on the training area – "B" company carried out musketry practices on the range – In the evening the Brigade Commander presided at a conference of all Commanding Officers, Adjutants, & all company commanders at LICQUES.	AJJ
– do –	18.		Weather fine – visibility good – Three companies carried out tactical training in the training area – "C" Company fired musketry practices on AUDREHEM Range.	AJJ
– do –	19.		Weather fine – visibility good – The Battalion took part in a Brigade attack scheme.	AJJ

WAR DIARY
or
INTELLIGENCE SUMMARY.
(Erase heading not required).

Army Form C. 2118.

Place	Date	Hour	Summary of Events and Information	Remarks and references to Appendices
IN BILLETS.	Sept 20		Weather fine - visibility good - Three companies carried out tactical training on Training Area and D company fire musketry practices during the day	App
"	21		Weather showery - visibility fair - Companies carried out interior economy and Drill	App
"	22		Weather showery - visibility fair - Voluntary divine Service were held during the morning. The day was occupied for Battalion Sports	App
"	23		The showery - The Battalion went out on attack scheme on the Training area during the day - C.O. officer and Co. to a hot Commanders attacked a scheme had to be shown commanders the camp of francais 10 A ... Sgt ... Brigade attack scheme	App MRII
"	24		Weather finer. The Battalion took part in a Brigade attack Scheme during the day on the Training area	

WAR DIARY
INTELLIGENCE SUMMARY.
(Erase heading not required.)

Army Form C. 2118.

Place	Date	Hour	Summary of Events and Information	Remarks and references to Appendices
IN BILLETS	1917 Sep 25		Weather fine. Battⁿ carried out training under Company arrangements. Riley the Authorise Range - Officers attended a demonstration of Platoon training by representatives of I.G.T. at LIGUES.	J.Y.
IN BILLETS	26		Weather fine. Battⁿ carried out a scheme on training area during the morning. Platoon training during the afternoon. Battalion transport moved to EUT of HUMONT.	J.Y.
IN BILLETS	27		Battalion entrained at BONNIERES at 4.30 am and 9.30 am. Guage to LUMBRES thence by French guage to PERINGHERST ROAD and marched to BILLETS at BRADHOEK, bombing at 9-4.5 pm. Weather - Raining.	J.Y.
IN FIELD	28		Battalion moved up to Assembly Area - WHITE CHATEAU AREA. Thence to Jumping off position in vicinity of HILL 60. - Thence attached in Support to the 26th ROYAL FUSILIERS and 10th QUEENS. R.W.S. Regt. A, B & C Coys. taking up positions on YPRES - COMMINES CANAL as Flank Guard as far as KORTEWILDE. Weather - Heavy rain. Casualties 2nd LT. LAX. evacuated N.Y.D.	J.Y.
-do-	29		Continued the attack as far as HOUTHEM. "D" Coy moving up to Canal, to complete Flank guard. "D" Coy mopped up HOUTHEM capturing 30 prisoners and 10 M.Gs. R.E. Stores etc. "D" Coy moved up on Right of Camp, Battⁿ relieved the Battalion not moved on Support Position 27 Bgde. Weather - Fair. Casualties Capt. AT. BROWNE. killed in action, 2nd Lt. PARKER. Wounded. 1 O.R. Killed, 3 Wounded. 1 Missing.	J.Y.

Army Form C. 2118.

WAR DIARY
or
INTELLIGENCE SUMMARY.
(Erase heading not required.)

Instructions regarding War Diaries and Intelligence Summaries are contained in F. S. Regs., Part II. and the Staff Manual respectively. Title pages will be prepared in manuscript.

Place	Date	Hour	Summary of Events and Information	Remarks and references to Appendices
In Field	Sept. 30		Battalion continued in the Attack, as Support Battalion to B. & D. Coys behind the 26.R.F.s. to Coy behind 10.Queens.R.W.S.- up to River Lys. (Wervicq-Comines). "C" Coy moved up in the night of 10.Queens.R.W.S, in the vicinity of Hospital Farm. Weather - Raining Casualties - O.R. 4 Wounded.	

SECRET.   20TH BN. DURHAM LIGHT INFANTRY.   Copy No.

APP I   ORDER NO. 91.

1.   The Battalion will hold the SCHERPENBERG - DICKEBUSCHE Lake Line from 28/ N.8.a.9.5. to N.7.c.4.0.

2.   Companies will independently tonight 31st August/1st Sept. to this Area, movement to commence at 3.30 a.m.

3.   Companies will be disposed in or in rear of the SCHERPENBERG - DICKEBUSCH LAKE Line as under:-

"A" Company - From N.8.a.9.5. to N.8.a.20.15.
"B" Company - From N.8.a.20.15 to N.7.d.7.6.
"C" Company - From N.7.d.7.6. to N.7.d.0.4.
"D" Company - From N.7.d.0.4. to N.7.c.4.0.

4.   Battalion Headquarters will be established at N.7.c.05.20 at 3.45 a.m.

5.   Companies will issue one bandolier to every man before moving.

6.   All Trench Stores etc. will be handed over to the Advance Parties of the 5th Bn. A & S Highlanders and receipts in duplicate forwarded to this office by noon 1st Sept.

7.   It is hoped that a hot breakfast will be available in the New Area.

8.   While in the New Area Companies will be at 30 minutes notice to move forward.

9.   Companies will report arrival in the New Area to New Bn. Headquarters as early as possible.

10.   ACKNOWLEDGE.

                    (SGD) F.W. PALEY,
                              Capt. & Adjutant,
1-9-18.   20th Bn. Durham Light Infantry.

Issued to Signals at 1.0 a.m.

Copy No. 1. O.C. "A" Company.
Copy No. 2. O.C. "B" Company.
Copy No. 3. O.C. "C" Company.
Copy No. 4. O.C. "D" Company.
Copy No. 5. O.C. Headquarters.
Copy No. 6. Quartermaster.
Copy No. 7. Transport Officer.
Copy No. 8. Medical Officer.
Copy No. 9. War Diary.
Copy No. 10. Filed.

SECRET.

60th Bn. DURHAM LIGHT INFANTRY.   COPY No........

ORDER No. 94.

APP II

Reference Map CALAIS 1/100,000.

1. INFORMATION. The enemy occupying the LA SOLIEURE SECTOR are expected to retire on the morning of the 23rd September.

2. INTENTION. The battalion is part of a force which is intended to follow up the retreating enemy and inflict as many casualties as possible and generally harass him. In addition he must be kept in touch.

3. DISPOSITIONS. The Battalion will form up as follows :-

    "A" Coy. Right Front Company.
    "B" "   Left Front Company.
    "C" "   Right Support Company.
    "D" "   Left Support Company.

Two platoons in front line and two in support in each Company.

4. BOUNDARIES. Boundaries as shown on map already issued to Companies.

5. OBJECTIVES. As shown on map already issued to Companies.

6. DIRECTION OF ADVANCE. From bearing of 112 degrees. Right of "B" Company will direct.

7. MACHINE GUNS. Two per Company in front line.

8. METHOD OF ADVANCE. By bounds. The front Companies advance on first bound (near edge of wood). The Support Companies move through to take second bound (original front Companies becoming Support Companies). Limit of second bound is further edge of wood. "A" and "B" Companies then leap frog "C" and "D" Companies to final objective (see map). Each bound will first be made good by scouts before Companies move forward.

9. ASSEMBLY POINT. Church - x roads.

10. ORDER OF MARCH. "C", "A", "D", "B" Companies and B.H.Q.

11. TIME. Head of the column will pass starting point at 9.30 a.m.

12. DRESS. Battle Order with caps.

13. TRANSPORT. Pack animals will not accompany the Battalion.

14. GENERAL. At 12 noon a bugler will sound the Regimental Call plus F G which is the signal for commencement of operations. Companies will rendezvous on the final objective at conclusion of operations which will be notified by the sounding of "Stand fast" on the bugle.
Company H.Q. will hoist a white signal flag and Battalion H.Q. a blue flag to show their locations. Battalion H.Q. will open at H.E.a.9.5. at 12 noon.

Captain & Adjutant.

Army Form C. 2118.

WAR DIARY
or
INTELLIGENCE SUMMARY.

(Erase heading not required.)

20th Bn. Durham, L.I.

Month: Nov 30

Place	Date Oct.	Hour	Summary of Events and Information	Remarks and references to Appendices
IN FIELD.	1.		Battalion laid in Support to 26" R.F.s & 10 "Queens" R.W.S. on WERVICQ – COMMINES LINE. – Weather fine. Visibility good. Casualties 3 O.R. Wounded.	J.Y.
- do -	2.		Battalion moved at 4-0 am to AMERIKA AREA, as Right Sup. Bn. Brigade in Reserve attacking MENIN. Remained there all day. Weather fair. Visibility moderate. Casualties Lt. G. ATKINSON & Lt. BLAIR, wounded. O.R. 1 killed, 2 wounded & 1 missing.	J.Y.
- do -	3.		Battalion remained in AMERIKA AREA until 6-30 p.m. Moved forward to GHELUWE, relieving 1st K.O.S.B. (29 Div) in the line. Relief completed at 2-0 am, 4th inst. Weather fine. Visibility good. Casualties. O.R. 1 Killed. 5 Wounded.	J.Y.
- do -	4.		Battalion held the line in front of GHELUWE. Weather dull. Visibility less. Casualties. 2 O.R. Wounded.	J.Y.
- do -	5.		At night Battalion was relieved by 24 "Queens" R.W.S. (24 Div.) Relief complete by 10-45 pm. Battalion then moved to Support area Du Bois Avenue R130 central sheet 28 and to Bevrona Rks. V130 sheet June. Visibility lost. 3 O.R. Wounded.	J.Y.

WAR DIARY
or
INTELLIGENCE SUMMARY.

(Erase heading not required.)

Army Form C. 2118.

Place	Date Oct.	Hour	Summary of Events and Information	Remarks and references to Appendices
In Bihucourt	6.		Battalion remained in Support at K.20 (Central). Interior Economy carried out so far as possible. Bivouacks improved. Weather fine. Visibility good. Casualties - O.R. 1 Killed 6 wounded	J.Y.
- do -	7.		Battalion was relieved during the afternoon by 23rd Batt. Middlesex Regt. (23rd Bde). Relief completed at 6.15 p.m. Weather fine. Visibility good. Batt. moved to vicinity of Helfaut Corner, to await entraining.	J.Y.
In Billets	8.		Entrained on Lorreys at 4.0 am for Stienacker. Thence marched to Bulltifs Bt K.24. c.3.3, Sheet 37. Fienvrheer Area. Remainder of day the Battalion rested. Weather hard.	J.Y.
- do -	9.		Interior Economy was carried out by Companies. Conference + recconna. to Commanding Officer, Adjutant + Coy Commanders at Bde H/Q.W.13.2.7. at 2.30 p.m. Weather fine.	J.Y.
- do -	10.		The Commanding Officer inspected Companies. 3 Companies started Platoon Training whilst one carried out - training area recconnoitred by Coy Commanders. Weather fine.	J.Y.

WAR DIARY
or
INTELLIGENCE SUMMARY

Army Form C. 2118.

Place	Date	Hour	Summary of Events and Information	Remarks and references to Appendices
IN BILLETS	Oct 11		Platoon Training & Bath. Scheme carried out. Remainder of Battalion bathed. Gas helmets inspected by Brigade Gas N.C.O. C of E Holy Communion Service (voluntary) held in Camp. Weather fine.	
do	12		Battalion took part in a Brigade attack scheme. Weather rainy	
Trenches	13		Battalion entrained at REMY SIDING N. at 11am and proceeded to STIRLING CASTLE by metre gauge railway and bivouacked in the vicinity of GLENCORSE TUNNELS. Advance parties proceeded to the assembly area by lorry and march route at 8pm for the laying of tapes. Battalion proceeded to assembly area (28-NW4) K35a 1.0 by march route at 11pm. Batt. HQ established at K.34.c.0.5.90. Weather showery.	
do	14		Battalion attacked at Zero 5.35am on true bearing 92°. Objective captured by 12 noon & Batt. HQ established at L.32.C.5.8. Patrols pushed forward immediately to effective being captured. Only slight resistance was encountered	

WAR DIARY
or
INTELLIGENCE SUMMARY.

Army Form C. 2118.

Place	Date	Hour	Summary of Events and Information	Remarks and references to Appendices
TRENCHES	17		9 field guns and 2 howitzers were captured. Also several M.Gs. Weather during the attack was very unfavourable, a heavy fog obscuring all view. Casualties 2nd Lt F Eden Bell M.Wound, Capt S Knott M.Wound, Lieut Hynes wounded. Rank & File 2 O.R. Wounded. 6 O.Rs killed. 60 O.Rs wounded.	A.1.
-do-	18		In continuance of previous days attack. Battalion pushed forward to the RIVER LYS. Battalion was relieved by the 2nd Batt Loyal North Lancashire Regt and proceeded to billets and bivouacs in K.34. Weather fine.	
-do-	19		Battalion proceeded by march route to the vicinity of MOORSEELE and occupied billets as part of Brigade in Reserve. Weather showery.	A.5.
BILLETS	19		The day was spent in cleaning of arms and equipment and reorganization of Platoons. Weather fine.	Nil.

Army Form C. 2118.

WAR DIARY
or
INTELLIGENCE SUMMARY.

(Erase heading not required)

Instructions regarding War Diaries and Intelligence Summaries are contained in F.S. Regs., Part II. and the Staff Manual respectively. Title pages will be prepared in manuscript.

Place	Date Oct	Hour	Summary of Events and Information	Remarks and references to Appendices
BILLETS	18.		Staff office. Reorganisation and change of arms & equipment. P.T. and arms drill occupied the day.	His
-do-	19		-ditto-	His
			6oy Bombers reconnoitre further ground in the vicinity of BISSEGHEM over RIVER LYS and afterwards return to same	His
-do-	20		Battalion moves by march route to billets in the vicinity of MARIONNETTERS.	His
-do-	21		Battalion took part in an attack at Zero 7.30am through the 36th Division. Objective being the RIVER ESCAUT on V.13 and V.19. Weather showery causing ground to be very heavy. On nearing the final objective considerable rifle and m.g. fire was very heavy. Enemy field guns were also very active. In spite of this the Battalion fought its way forward in clusters of 6 or so. On account of weight and exceptionally heavy m.g. fire from left flank and rear	His

(A7092) Wt W12899/M1293. 75,000. 1/17. D.D. & L., Ltd. Forms/C.2118/14.

WAR DIARY
or
INTELLIGENCE SUMMARY.

Army Form C. 2118.

Place	Date	Hour	Summary of Events and Information	Remarks and references to Appendices
TRENCHES	21		Think being extended for a distance of about 3000x advance finds our route along the line K.12.c.5.8 to U.5.c.5.3. Left coming to captured POELDRIESCH and attacked the from U.18.a.3.6 along road to U.12.c.6.5. This line was consolidated during the night and patrols were pushed forward. Casualties. 2nd Lieut. T.W. ARMSTRONG — KILLED — 2nd Lieut T Wood and 2nd LIEUT S.W.WARWICK wounded. 20 ORs killed & 46 ORs wounded.	A/25
-do-	22		Line captured on 21st was strengthened and the men looked forward frequently so as to locate enemy posts for artillery targets.	A/25
-do-	23		Battalion was relieved by 1st/4th Battn Bedn Regt and proceeded to billets at 29.S.W.O.8 and took up position of Support Battalion to the Brigade. Scouts kept in touch.	A/25
BILLETS	24		Battalion remained in Support and carried out programme of etc. Advance parties proceeded to assembly area and took over trenches there.	

Place	Date	Hour	Summary of Events and Information	Remarks and references to Appendices
TRENCHES	22		Battalion moved to assembly area at ZERO 9am when they attacked with the objective of RIVER ESCAUT as right Battalion of the Brigade. Very heavy fighting was experienced immediately South of KATTESTRAAT. R.R. Battalion fought its way up to the line of the road in R.R. Owing to the left flank being exposed our advance was retired. Many casualties were inflicted on the enemy in our left flank by Lewis guns. Several M.Gs were captured. Owing to casualties 10th Batn Queens R.R. Army reinforced both our flanks. On positions were consolidated at 6.30 P.M. 6.3.9 R.7.P.19.6.41. Forward and completed. During the right advance Casualties - 2nd Lieut W.HEBRON & 2nd Lieut DLAX killed Captain F.WILKINSON, M.C. 2nd Lieut T.APPLETON and Lieut WOOD, M.C. and 2nd Lieut F.A.DONNELLY wounded. Killed and 111 wounded. 22 OR's	A.S. A.D.

WAR DIARY
or
INTELLIGENCE SUMMARY.

Army Form C. 2118.

Place	Date	Hour	Summary of Events and Information	Remarks and references to Appendices
TRENCHES	Oct 26		Information was received from civilians that enemy was retiring in consequence patrols were pushed forward during the morning and reached AVELGEM which was reported clear of enemy at 10 am. During the afternoon a strong patrol who pushed forward to establish posts in RUGGE LANGESTRAAT and AVELGEM and OOSTENDE. Ghe patrol established posts at AVELGEM and LANGESTRAAT int'n account of enemy keeping up fire on the road to establish posts at RUGGE and OOSTENDE. 10th Batt. Queens R W Surrey Regt relieved this patrol and on completion of this relief the Battalion moved to billets in SOUTH - COURTRAI. Weather fine.	A/1
BILLETS	27.		Weather fine – Battalion carried out cleaning of arms and equipment and reorganisation	A/1
-do-	28		ditto	A/1
-do-	29.		ditto A/er officers arrived and took command of Bn. Maj R W Gardiner handed to D Booth	A/1

WAR DIARY
or
INTELLIGENCE SUMMARY.

Army Form C. 2118.

Place	Date	Hour	Summary of Events and Information	Remarks and references to Appendices
BILLETS	Oct 30		Weather fine. Battalion carried out inspections and training	Apt
"	31		Weather fine during day - showery at night. Platoon training was carried out during the morning and sports during the afternoon	Apt

Samuel Lt Col
Commdg. 20 Durham L.I.

1/10/18

Army Form C. 2118.

WAR DIARY
or
INTELLIGENCE SUMMARY.

20th Bn. Durham. Light. Inf.

(Erase heading not required.)

Instructions regarding War Diaries and Intelligence Summaries are contained in F. S. Regs., Part II. and the Staff Manual respectively. Title pages will be prepared in manuscript.

Place	Date	Hour	Summary of Events and Information	Remarks and references to Appendices
TRENCHES	1918 Nov. 1		Battalion moved by march route to KROTE area, where dinners were served. Battalion relieved 1 coy Lanc Fusiliers (1/4th) 1 coy 18th Lancs Fusiliers and 2 coys 19th Durham L.I. along RIVER ESCAUT front in the vicinity of TERHOVE and KERHOVE. Weather fine. Casualties:— 5 O.R's wounded.	Fair
—do—	2		Weather fine. Front was patrolled and the Enemy artillery was active on Battalion forward sector throughout the day. Casualties 5 ORs wounded 1 OR killed	Fair
—do—	3		Weather cloudy and showery at night. 2 L.G. posts were established on enemy side of RIVER ESCAUT but owing to enemy's attempts to cut them they were withdrawn without casualties. Casualties:— 3 O.R's. wounded + 2 ORs killed.	Fair
—do—	4		Weather fine. Battalion was relieved by the 11th Battn. Queen's R.W. Surrey Regiment and on completion of relief Battalion moved to VICHTE AREA to billets. Casualties 1 OR killed 2 OR wounded.	Fair

WAR DIARY
or
INTELLIGENCE SUMMARY.
(Erase heading not required.)

Army Form C. 2118.

Instructions regarding War Diaries and Intelligence Summaries are contained in F. S. Regs., Part II. and the Staff Manual respectively. Title pages will be prepared in manuscript.

Place	Date Nov.	Hour	Summary of Events and Information	Remarks and references to Appendices
BILLETS	5.		Weather showery — Companies carried out reorganisation of platoons and cleaning of arms and equipment.	Apt.
— do —	6.		Weather rainy — Companies carried out reorganisation etc. also Physical Drill and Arms Drill. Baths were allotted to Bath.	Apt.
— do —	7.		Weather mild — showery — Companies completed bathing — Companies were practised in crossing a river by Cringes and boats in view of an attack across RIVER ESCAUT.	Apt.
— do —	8.		Weather heavy rain fell throughout the day — "Jamming up" across river was practised.	Apt.
— do —	9.		Weather fine — Battalion moved to the vicinity of KLEINE BERG — news received during morning that enemy had retired from eastern bank of RIVER ESCAUT as a consequence the Battalion occupied billets at MEERSCHE.	Apt. APP 1

Army Form C. 2118.

WAR DIARY
or
INTELLIGENCE SUMMARY.
(Erase heading not required.)

Instructions regarding War Diaries and Intelligence Summaries are contained in F. S. Regs., Part II. and the Staff Manual respectively. Title pages will be prepared in manuscript.

Place	Date Nov.	Hour	Summary of Events and Information	Remarks and references to Appendices
BILLETS.	10.		Weather fine - Battalion moved by march route to SCHOORISSE were billets were occupied -	
—do—	11.		Weather fine during morning, showery remainder of day - Battalion continuing in pursuit of the enemy passed through 123rd Brigade and formed an advance guard to the 124th. Brigade. Message received about 10 a.m. that an Armistice was signed and that hostilities would cease at 11 a.m.; as a consequence the Battalion occupied billets in the vicinity of NEDERBRAKEL. An outpost line was formed East of Nederbrakel. 1 O.R. accidently wounded whilst on outpost duty.	
—do—	12.		Weather fine - Battalion moved to OUDENKERKENHOEK + occupied billets in the vicinity.	
—do—	13.		Weather fine - "C" Coy formed an outpost line on the northern boundary of the Brigade - Remaining companies carried out drill a b d reorganization	

Army Form C. 2118.

WAR DIARY
or
INTELLIGENCE SUMMARY.
(Erase heading not required.)

Place	Date	Hour	Summary of Events and Information	Remarks and references to Appendices
BILLETS.	Nov. 14		Weather fine – Companies carried out reorganisation, cleaning of arms and equipment and close order drill	
– do –	15.		Weather fine – Companies carried out close order drill and inspections. "D" Coy. relieved "B" Coy. in the Outpost system	
– do –	16.		Weather fine – "D" Coy. were relieved in the Outpost system by a Coy. of 18th Bn. K.R.R.C. – "A" Coy. relieved a Coy. of 26th Bn. Royal Fusiliers in the Brigade Outpost system. "B" Coy. carried out close order drill and inspections	
– do –	17.		Weather fine – Brigadier inspected the Battalion in fighting order – Voluntary non-Conformist Service held at 6 pm	
– do –	18.		Weather cold – slight snow during the day. Battalion moved by march route to the vicinity of POELAERE – "B" Coy. occupied an outpost position in the vicinity of NEYGHEM –	APP 11
– do –	19.		Weather fine – Battalion carried out inspection parades – Platoon and company drill.	

Army Form C. 2118.

WAR DIARY
or
INTELLIGENCE SUMMARY.
(Erase heading not required.)

Instructions regarding War Diaries and Intelligence Summaries are contained in F. S. Regs., Part II. and the Staff Manual respectively. Title pages will be prepared in manuscript.

Place	Date	Hour	Summary of Events and Information	Remarks and references to Appendices
BILLETS	20		Weather misty & cold – Battalion moved by march route to the vicinity of BEVENE –	
– do –	21.		Weather misty & cold – Battalion carried out inspections and Platoon and Coy. Drill – The afternoon was occupied in Recreational Games	
– do –	22		Weather fine – During the morning inspections, platoon and coy drill were carried out – In the afternoon recreational training	
– do –	23		Weather fine – During the morning inspections, platoon and coy. drill were carried out – In the afternoon recreational training	
– do –	24.		Battalion attended Church Service during the morning – In the afternoon the Battalion football team played a team of 26th R.F. Result – 26th R.F. 3 – 20th D.L.I. Weather fine but misty.	
– do –	25.		Weather fine – Battalion carried out inspections, platoon & company drill – Recreational Training in the afternoon	

WAR DIARY
or
INTELLIGENCE SUMMARY.
(Erase heading not required.)

Army Form C. 2118.

Place	Date NOV	Hour	Summary of Events and Information	Remarks and references to Appendices
BILLETS.	26.		Weather fine – Battalion carried out inspections, platoon, coy. & open order guard drill – In the afternoon recreational training was carried out.	A.J.
– do –	27.		Weather fine – Battalion carried out inspections, platoon, coy. and open order guard drill – In the afternoon recreational training was carried out – C & D coys. played each other in the first phase of the Divisional Football Tournament – "D" coy. won by 2 goals to one.	A.J.
– do –	28		Weather broken – Battalion carried out a short Route March in the neighbourhood of Bièvène. In the afternoon recreational training was carried out. A & B coys. played each other in the first phase of the Divisional Football Tournament – "B" coy. won by 2 goals to nil.	%

WAR DIARY
or
INTELLIGENCE SUMMARY.

(Erase heading not required.)

Army Form C.-2118.

Place	Date	Hour	Summary of Events and Information	Remarks and references to Appendices
BILLETS	Nov. 29		Weather - dull but dry. Battalion carried out inspections, platoon, coy. and open order drill. In the afternoon recreational training was carried out. A concert was given by the "CRUMPS" DIV. CONCERT PARTY in the evening	96./
- do -	30		Weather - cold & dry. Battalion carried out a short ROUTE MARCH in neighbourhood of BIÉVÈNE. In the afternoon a football match was played between "B" & "D" resulting in a win for "D" of 5 goals to 1. "D" Coy. will therefore represent the Bn. in the Inter. Coy. Divisional Football Tournament.	96./

Arthur Hayes Lt. Col.
Commdg. 20/B Durham L.I.

SECRET.   20TH BN. DURHAM LIGHT INFANTRY ORDER NO.99.   Copy No..

Reference Map - Sheet 29.

1. The Battalion will relieve part of the 11th Bn. "Queens" R.W.S. Regt. in the line tonight. After relief Companies will be disposed as follows:-
Right Front Coy. - "B" Coy.   Left Front Coy. - "C" Coy.
Right Support Coy. - "A" Coy. Left Support Coy. - "D" Coy.
The two front Companies will have two platoons in front and two in Support. Further details as to the Companies of the 11th Bn. "Queens" R.W.S. Regt. to be relieved will be issued later.

2. After relief Battalion Headquarters will be located at KERK HOVE CHATEAU - Q.14.b.9.3.

3. The Battalion will march to the Line by stages i.e. halting in the area J.33.a & b, J.34.a & c for dinner.
   Starting Point - Cross Roads I.17.c.7.3.
   Time of passing S.P. - Head of Column to pass S.P. 11.00 hours.
Order of March - "B", "C", H.Q., "D", "A" Companies.
Dress - Battle Order (without blanket or great-coat)
Route - S.P. - J.25.a.1.8. - J.19.c.9.2. - J.25.b.8.4. - J.26.d.3.4. - J.26.d.8.8.

The Battalion will be clear of the staging area by 16.00 hours.

4. All blankets will be rolled in bundles of 10 and securely labelled. All great-coats and caps will be put in packs.
Blankets and packs will be stacked outside Coy. H.Qrs. as near as possible to the main road by 10.00 hours.
Officers Valises and Mess Kits will be stacked at the same dumps by the same time. Company Commanders will detail two men from "Details" left out of the line to act as guard over these dumps.

5. Company Commanders horses will report to Companies at 10.30 hours.

6. Lewis Gun Limbers will report to Companies at 08.30 hours, and will move immediately behind Companies leading platoon. 1 limber will also report to Bn. H.Q. Mess at 10.30 hours. The Maltese Cart will report to the Aid Post at 10.00 hours.
Cookers will accompany the Battalion to the staging Area where a hot meal will be served.

7. Rations for consumption on the 10th inst. will be issued today and carried to the line on the man.

8. All details left out of the line will parade at the Transport Lines at 11.00 hours. They will move with "B" Echelon when it moves to new location. The senior N.C.O. will take charge of the party.

9. On arrival in the line and after relief is complete Companies will send two good runners to Bn. Headquarters for duty until after commencement of operations.

10. Completion of relief will be reported by sending O.K. to this office.

11. ACKNOWLEDGE.

                          (SGD) F.W. PALEY, Capt. & Adjutant,
9-10-18.   20th Bn. Durham Light Infantry.

Copy No. 1. O.C. "A" Company.   Copy No. 6. Medical Officer.
      " 2. O.C. "B" Company.   "   7. O.C. H. Qrs.
      " 3. O.C. "C" Company.   "   8. H.Q. Mess.
      " 4. O.C. "D" Company.   "   9. File.
      "   T.O. & Q.M.   " 10. War Diary.

SECRET. Copy No.....

20th BN. DURHAM LIGHT INFANTRY ORDER NO. 101.

Reference Maps - TOURNAI 1/100,000.
BRUSSELS (To be issued later)

INFORMATION.

In accordance with the terms of the Armistice, the occupied portions of France, Belgium and Luxemberg are to be evacuated by the enemy by the 26th November 1918. A further withdrawal East of the Rhine will take place on a later date.

The Second Army, consisting of the Cavalry Corps (less 1 Division) 11, 111 and XX11 and Canadian Corps will begin its advance to German Frontier on November 17th 1918.
The Cavalry Corps will cover the advance, and be followed by the Canadian Corps on the Right and 11 Corps on left, one day's march in rear.

On November 17th, the Cavalry Corps will advance through the present outpost line by the following roads:-
RENAIX - ELLEGELLES = LESSINES.

The approximate Outpost Line to be taken up by the 41st Division is to be the ENGHIEN - NINOVE Road from 1 mile N. of ENGHIEN to the Southern Outskirts of NINOVE.
Dividing Line between 124th and 123rd Infantry Brigades in the Outpost Line will be Kilometre 9 on ENGHIEN - NINOVE Road.

124th Infantry Brigade will be covered by an advance guard of 1 Coy. 1/1st Yorks Cyclist Regt.
During the advance of the Advanced Guard will maintain touch with the advanced troops of the formations on our right and left.

On arrival on the NINOVE - ENGHIEN Road the Advance Guard will at once take up an Outpost Line, picqueting all roads entering the area from an Easterly direction until relieved by the 26th Bn. Royal Fusiliers and 20th Bn. Durham Light Infantry as detailed in para. 4.

DISCIPLINE.

March discipline must be the object of Special attention.
The following points require particular notice:-

(a) Halts will take place from 10 minutes to every clock hour to the clock hour, whatever time units may have passed the starting point. Unit and Company Commanders should synchronise their watches so that men are ready fallen in at the clock hour, and the whole column steps off together.

(b) In Artillery and Units marching with Transport, a warning will be given a few minutes before each halt to ensure that all vehicles are well into the side of the road when the halt is given.

(c) No officers or other ranks will march alongside the column, but must be in the intervals. If they have occasion to pass from front to rear of a column they will do so on the right hand side.

(d) Any personnel marching with Transport will be formed in bodies.

(f) On paved roads lorries and cars must be given way to and must not be turned off the pave.
will
(g) Troops/marching with rifles slung over one shoulder, arms will be brought to the trail on the command "march to attention", but this command will only be given on arrival in billets and as a compliment on passing the Divisional, Corps or Army Commanders for the first time on any day.

Marching through towns and large villages troops will be given the command "march at attention with arms slung" when all rifles will be slung on the left shoulder, march in other respectes as when marching at attention.

(h) There are not restrictions as to smoking when marching at "Ease".

INTENTION.

1. The Battalion will move on the 18th inst. probably to the POLLAERE Area.

2. At 5.0 a.m. on the 18th inst. all Outposts found by the Battalion will be withdrawn to their Companies.

3. The Head of the Battalion will pass H.Q. Mess at 08.00 hours.
Order of March - "B", "A", "H.Q.", "C" & "D" Companies.
DRess - Fighting Order with caps. Steel helmets to be carried.
Route - IDEGHEM - GRIMMINGHE - SANTBERGEN - NIEUWENHOVE.

4. O.C. "B" Company will be required to take over that part of the Outposts between DENDERWINDEKE (inclusive) to Kilometre 9 i.e. Brigade Right Boundary, from the Cyclist Company tomorrow. A liaison post at Kilometre 9 will be established with the 123rd Infantry Brigade. "B" Company will be billeted in this area to conform to the Outpost Line. The Commanding Officer will arrange all further details with O.C. "B" Company tomorrow, 18th inst.
    As soon as relief of the Outposts is completed, notification to this effect will be immediately sent to Battalion Headquarters.

5. A Billeting Party consisting of 2/Lieut. H.WHITFIELD, 1 N.C.O. from H.Q. and 1 N.C.O. per Company will parade with bicycles at H.Q. Mess at a time to be notified later. This party will carry all arms and equipment (Battle Order).

6. All officers' valises, except those of "B" Company, will be stacked outside each Company H.Qrs. not later than 06.45 hours. Company Mess Kits will be carried on the Field Kitchens. The Officers' Mess Cart will report at H.Q. at 07.15 hours. The Maltese Cart will report at the R.A.P. at 06.45 hours.
    "B" Company's kit will be stacked opposite the R.A.P.
    All blankets will be rolled in bundles of 10 and securely labelled and stacked at Company Kit Dumps by 06.45 hours.

7. Companies will forward each evening without fail usual billeting lists which should reach this office not later than 20.00.

8. O's.C. Companies will arrange from now onwards for a sentry to be posted on each group of billets. During the march Companies will arrabge for a company Alarm Post to be established and a Battalion Alarm Post will be notified each day. Any prisoners of war found in Billeting Areas will be sent to the Quartermaster, who will arrange to billet and feed them. The Quartermaster will notify this Office as early as possible each day the number of P.of W. accomodated by him. Instructions as to their further disposal will be issued later.
    Mens' packs will only be issued at the two days' halts. O.C. Companies for men to carry cleaning kit etc. in their haversacks.
    Officers' valises will not be delivered to Officers except at the two days' halts. In view of this Officers will arrange to carry necessary articles in a trench bundle which will be carried on Company L.G. Limbers.

9. ACKNOWLEDGE.

(SGD) F.W. PALEY,
Captain & Adjutant,
20th Bn. Durham Light Infantry.

17-11-18.

SECRET.   20TH BN. DURHAM LIGHT INFANTRY ORDER NO.102.   Copy No.

Reference Maps - BRUSSELS & TOURNAI 1/100,000.

1. The Battalion will move today to BIEVENE (see TOURNAI Map).
2. Order of March - "C","D", H.Q., "A" & "B" Companies.
   Starting Point for all except "B" Company will be X Roads South of P in POLLAERE (see BRUSSELS Map).
   Time - Head of column tom pass S.P. at 07.30 hours.
   Route - S.P., DENDERWINDEKE - HERINNE - HERHOUT.
   Dress - Fighting Order with Caps.

3. B Company will join the column at road junction just NORTH of the C in VECHEM, (i.e. 1 mile south of DENDERWINDEKE) at 08.38 hours.

4. A billeting party consisting of 2/Lieut. H.WHITFIELD and 1 N.C.O. from "A", "C" & "D" Companies and 2 from H.Q. will rendezvous at Orderly Room with bicycle etc. at 08.00 hours.

5. All packs, blankets and surplus stores will be dumped under a guard at the following points :- A,C & D Companies at each Coy. H.Q. Battalion H.Q. at Orderly Room, B Coy. one dump on main road (NINIVE - BRUSSELS) at X Roads jost N. of 9 in Kilometre 19. 1 dump at Coy. H.Q. and 1 dump at 1st X Roads on NEYGHEM - LENNICK ST.QUENTIN Road just N. of Y in DRY.

5. A running is meetinf lorries at 08.00 hours at DENDERWINDEKE Church and will conduct them to the Q.M. Stores. Permission has been asked for lorries to make a second jouerney if required. Q.M. will be informed later if successful.

6. Officers' valises will be stacked outside Coy. H.Qrs. of A,C & D Companies by 06.30 hours. Mess Cart will report to H.Q. Mess at 06.45 hours. B Companies valises will be stacked with the remaining Kit.

7. ACKNOWLEDGE.

(Sgd) F.W. PALEY, Capt. & Adjutant,
20th Bn. Durham Light Infantry.

Copy No. 1.   Filed.
Copy No. 2.   O.C. "A" Company.
Copy No. 3.   O.C. "B" Company.
Copy No. 4.   O.C. "C" Company.
Copy No. 5.   O.C. "D" Company.
Copy No. 6.   O.C. H.Qrs.
Copy No. 7.   Quartermaster.
Copy No. 8.   Transport Officer.
Copy No. 9.   Medical Officer.
Copy No. 10.   R.S.M.
Copy No. 11.   War Diary.

WAR DIARY or INTELLIGENCE SUMMARY

Army Form C. 2118.

20th Durham Light Infantry

Place	Date Dec.	Hour	Summary of Events and Information	Remarks and references to Appendices
"BILLETS" BIÉVÈNE	1		DIVINE SERVICE was held in the forenoon in the village hall. Weather – fine but cold.	J.G.
– do –	2		Weather - fine. In the forenoon battalion carried out a Route March of 8 mls. in the neighbourhood of billets. Recreational training was carried out by companies in the afternoon.	J.G.
– do –	3		Weather – showery. In the forenoon Platoon, Coy and Battalion drill was carried out. The afternoon was devoted to Recreational training.	J.G.
– do –	4		Weather - fine. Battalion carried out Platoon & Coy Drill in forenoon. The afternoon was devoted to Recreational training. In the evening June French Classes for the men were started. Over 60 men attended.	J.G.
– do –	5		Weather - fine. Battalion carried out a Route March in the neighbourhood of billets in the forenoon. The afternoon was devoted to Recreational training. The French Classes met again in the evening.	J.G.

WAR DIARY
or
INTELLIGENCE SUMMARY.
(Erase heading not required.)

Army Form C. 2118.

Instructions regarding War Diaries and Intelligence Summaries are contained in F. S. Regs., Part II. and the Staff Manual respectively. Title pages will be prepared in manuscript.

Place	Date Dec.	Hour	Summary of Events and Information	Remarks and references to Appendices
BILLETS BIÉVÈNE	6		Weather – fine. The morning was spent in Platoon & Coy. Drill. Cross country runs were organized in the afternoon. In the evening the French classes were held.	J.C.
– do –	7		Weather – dull. In the forenoon Companies went to Viane for baths, and kit inspections were held. The second phase of the Divisional Tournament was played between "D" Coy. of ours & "A" Coy. 26th R.F. "D" Coy. won by 2 goals to nil.	J.C.
– do –	8		Weather – exceptionally fine. Divine Services for all denominations were held in the Village Hall. In the afternoon a football match was arranged between the Officers 26th D.L.I. + the Officers 26th R.F. Score :– D.L.I. 6 goals. R.F. nil.	J.C.
– do –	9		Weather – dull. In the morning Platoon & Coy. Drill was carried out. Inter-Platoon Football Tournament (Battalion) was started, + recreational training was held in the afternoon. The French classes met in the evening.	J.C.

Army Form C. 2118.

WAR DIARY
or
INTELLIGENCE SUMMARY.
(Erase heading not required.)

Instructions regarding War Diaries and Intelligence Summaries are contained in F. S. Regs., Part II. and the Staff Manual respectively. Title pages will be prepared in manuscript.

Place	Date Dec	Hour	Summary of Events and Information	Remarks and references to Appendices
BILLETS BIÉNÉNE	10		Weather - cold and raw. In the forenoon the battalion carried out a Route March in the neighbourhood. The Inter-Platoon Battalion Football Tournament was continued in the afternoon. In the evening the FRENCH CLASSES were held.	J.b.
- do -	11		Weather - showery. In the battalion carried out Kit Inspection prior to moving. A Cross Country Race was held in the afternoon.	J.b.
BILLETS ENGHIEN	12		Weather - wet and stormy. The battalion moved by Route March via PUDGT to ENGHIEN arriving shortly after 1200 hrs.	J.b APP.I
BILLETS HAL	13		Weather - fine. The battalion moved by Route March to HAL and remained in billets for the night.	J.b APP ii
BILLETS WATERLOO	14		Weather - fine. The battalion moved by Route March via HAL STATION X Roads 400 yds. S.E. of BUYSINGHEM STATION - TOURNEPPE to WATERLOO arriving there at 1230 hrs	J.b. APP iii
BILLETS - WATERLOO	15		DIVINE SERVICE was held in a hall in the village. The men visited the battlefield at MONT ST. JEAN in the afternoon and saw the "LION". Weather - fine.	J.b.

WAR DIARY
or
INTELLIGENCE SUMMARY.

(Erase heading not required.)

Army Form C. 2118.

Place	Date DEC.	Hour	Summary of Events and Information	Remarks and references to Appendices
BILLETS GENAPPE	16		Weather - fine. The battalion proceeded by ROUTE MARCH to GENAPPE and was inspected on the line of march by KING ALBERT, the King of the Belgians, 2 KILOMETRES N. of GENAPPE.	APP IV /c
BILLETS LIGNY	17		Weather - fine. The battalion proceeded by ROUTE MARCH to LIGNY via QUATRE BRAS, arriving in LIGNY at 1215 hrs.	APP V /c
BILLETS SPY	18		Weather - wet and stormy. The battalion proceeded by ROUTE MARCH to SPY via SOIGNÉE — ST. MARTIN, arriving at 1200 hrs.	APP VI /c
BILLETS CHAMPION	19		Weather - fine but gusty. The battalion continued the march and proceeded via NAMUR to CHAMPION arriving at 1430 hrs.	APP VII /c
BILLETS ANTHEIT	20		Weather - wet and stormy. The battalion completed the march proceeding via WANZE to ANTHEIT & arriving there at 1400 hrs. Billets were found and each Coy. given a Coy. Mess for the men. The school beside the Church was taken over for Educational Purposes.	/c

Army Form C. 2118.

WAR DIARY
or
INTELLIGENCE SUMMARY.
(Erase heading not required.)

Place	Date	Hour	Summary of Events and Information	Remarks and references to Appendices
BILLETS ANTHEIT	DEC 21		Weather - windy. The battalion settled down into Winter Billets in the morning. In the afternoon recreational training was carried out.	J.6.
- do -	22		Weather - very wet and stormy. DIVINE SERVICES were held in the LECTURE ROOM of the SCHOOL for C.E. men and mass was attended by R.C.s at the convent. In the evening a Lecture on "Charles Dickens" was delivered to a big audience in the Agricultural Hall, WANZE.	J.6.
- do -	23		Weather - wet and stormy. In the morning Companies carried out Interior Economy work. The afternoon was spent in recreational training.	J.6.
- do -	24		Weather - fine. In the morning a large draft of minors was sent home for demobilization. Preparations for the Christmas Dinner were attended to in the afternoon and evening.	J.6.
- do -	25		Weather - fine. Each Company had a huge Christmas Dinner in the middle of the day, following DIVINE SERVICE which was held in the SCHOOL LECTURE ROOM in the morning. Revelry and rejoicing continued till late in the evening.	J.6.

Army Form C. 2118.

WAR DIARY
or
INTELLIGENCE SUMMARY.
(Erase heading not required.)

Instructions regarding War Diaries and Intelligence Summaries are contained in F. S. Regs., Part II. and the Staff Manual respectively. Title pages will be prepared in manuscript.

Place	Date	Hour	Summary of Events and Information	Remarks and references to Appendices
BILLETS ANTHEIT	DEC 26		Weather - showery. In the morning the SCHOOL ROOMS were prepared for the continuation of the EDUCATIONAL CLASSES. Recreational training was carried out in the afternoon. A football match between an OFFICERS' TEAM and a NON. COM. OFFICERS' TEAM resulted in a win of 4-0 for the OFFICERS.	do.
- do -	27		Weather - showery. In the morning the SCHEME OF CLASSES for the men was explained to all companies. Recreational Training was carried out in the afternoon. An OFFICERS' FRENCH class met in the evening.	do.
- do -	28		Weather - wet. In the morning billets were inspected by the General Officer Commanding 124 Inf. Bde. Group.	do.
- do -	29		Weather - wet and stormy. DIVINE SERVICE was held in the morning for all denominations.	do.
- do -	30		Weather - showery. Classes in READING, WRITING, SPELLING, ARITHMETIC, ENGLISH GRAMMAR, ENGLISH COMPOSITION, FRENCH were held in the morning. Recreational training was carried out in the afternoon.	do.
- do -	31		Weather - fine and dry. Classes met again in the morning. Recreational training was carried out in the afternoon.	do.

Arthur Raye? Lt. Col.
Commdg. 20 Durham L.I.

APP. I

SECRET.   20th BN. DURHAM LIGHT INFANTRY ORDER NO. 102.   Copy No....

Reference Maps - BRUSSELS & TOURNAI 1/100,000.

1. **INTENTION.** The Battalion will move from its present area tomorrow, 12th December 1918 and will proceed to ENGHIEN.

2. **INSTRUCTIONS.**

(a) The Battalion will parade on the Battalion Football Ground at 07.30 hours. Markers will report to the R.S.M. on the ground at 07.15 hours.

(b) DRESS - FULL MARCHING ORDER.

ROUTE - BIEVENE - PUDOT - KILO 12.

(c) DISTANCES. The following distances will be maintained on the march :-

```
        Between Battalions    -  100 yards.
        Between Companies     -   10 yards.
        Between rear Coy. &
          Transport.          -   10 yards.
        After every 12th
          vehicle             -   10 yards.
```

(e) REAR PLATOON - O.C. "D" Company will detail one platoon to march in rear of the Brigade Group according to instructions already issued.

3. **TRANSPORT.**
Lewis Gun Limbers. Lewis Gun limbers will report to Companies at 16.00 hours today.

Medical Cart.   The Medical Cart will report to the R.A.P. at 06.00 hours tomorrow.

MESS CART.   Mess Cart will report to H.Q. Mess at 06.45 hours tomorrow.

4. **BLANKETS.** Blankets will be rolled according to the method already shown to C.Q.M.S's by the Quartermaster, and stacked outside Company H.Q. by 06.30 hours. Each Company will leave 1 man (unable to march) in charge of the dump. Blankets will be collected by lorry after the departure of the Battalion.

5. **OFFICERS KITS.** Officers' valises of H.Q., "A" & "B" Coys will be stacked outside Orderly Room by 06.30 hours. Those of "C" & "D" Companies will be stacked with the Company Blankets for collection by lorry. Mess Kits will be carried on the Field Kitchens.

6. **ACKNOWLEDGE.**

(sgd) L.W. SHEPHERDSON,
Capt. A/Adjutant,
20th Bn. Durham Light Infantry.

11-12-18.

Copy No. 1. Filed.
Copy No. 2. O.C. "A" Company.
Copy No. 3. O.C. "B" Company.
Copy No. 4. O.C. "C" Company.
Copy No. 5. O.C. "D" Company.
Copy No. 6. O.C. H.Q.
Copy No. 7. Quartermaster.
Copy No. 8. Transport Officer.
Copy No. 9. Medical Officer.
Copy No. 10. R.S.M.   Copy No. 11. WAR DIARY.

SECRET.  Copy.No....

20TH BN. DURHAM LIGHT INFANTRY ORDER No.104.

Reference Map - BRUSSELS 1/100,000.

1. **INTENTION.** The Battalion will continue the march tomorrow the 13th inst. and will proceed to Hal.

2. **INSTRUCTIONS.** The Battalion will parade in column of route on the road outside the Battalion Billet at 08.45 hours, with the Head of Column outside the Eastern Gate of the Billet.

    Order of March - "B","C","D","A" Coys. H.Q. & Transport.

    DRESS - Full Marching Order.

    ROUTE. - Direct.

    DISTANCES. - Same distances will be maintained as today.

3. **TRANSPORT.** Lewis Gun Limbers and Medical Cart will report at the Battalion Billet by 08.00 hours.
    Mess Cart will report to H.Q. Mess by 08.15 hours.

4. **BLANKETS.** Blankets will be stacked outside the billet in Company dumps by 07.30 hours and 1 man left in charge of each dump.

5. **OFFICERS KITS.** The Officers Kits of H.Q. "A" & "B" Coys will be stacked outside their respective Headquarters by 07.30 hours. Those of "C" & "D" Coys. will be stacked with the Company blankets. Mess Kits will be carried on the Field Kitchens.

6. **BILLETING.** Arrangements will be notified later.

7. **ACKNOWLEDGE.**

(Signed) S. Shepherdson.
Captain, A/Adjutant.
20th Bn, DURHAM LIGHT INFANTRY.

12-12-1918.

Copy No. 1.   Filed.
Copy No. 2.   O.C. "A" Coy.
Copy No. 3.   O.C. "B" Coy.
Copy No. 4.   O.C. "C" Coy.
Copy No. 5.   O.C. "D" Coy.
Copy No. 6.   O.C. H.Q.
Copy No. 7.   Quartermaster.
Copy No. 8.   Transport Officer.
Copy No. 9.   Medical Officer.
Copy No.10.   R.S.M.
Copy No.11.   War Diary.

APP III

SECRET.   Copy......1...

20th BN. DURHAM LIGHT INFANTRY ORDER NO. 103.

Reference Map - 1/100,000. BRUSSELS.

1. **INTENTION.** The Battalion will continue its march tomorrow the 14th inst. and will proceed to the WATERLOO area.

2. **INSTRUCTIONS.** The Battalion will parade in Column of Route on the road outside the Battalion Billet at 08.00 hours ready to move off at 08.15 hours. The Head of the Column will be at the junction of this road with the HAL-TUBIZE Road.

ORDER OF MARCH. "C" "D" "A" Coys. H.Q. "B" Coy. and Transport.

DRESS. - Full Marching Order.

ROUTE - HAL STATION - X ROADS 400 yards S.E. of BUYSINGHEM STATION - TOURNEPPE - road junction on BRUSSELS - BRAINE L'ALLEUD Road at Kilo 10 thence South.

DISTANCES.- Same distances will be maintained as today.

3. **TRANSPORT.** Medical Cart will report to the R.A.P. at 07.30 hours. Mess Cart will report to H.Q. Mess at 07.30 hours.

4. **BLANKETS.** Blankets will be stacked outside the billet in Company dumps by 07.30 hours and 1 man left in charge of each dump.

5. **OFFICERS KITS.** The Officers Kits of H.Q. "A" & "B" Coys. will be stacked outside their respective Headquarters by 07.15 hours. Those of "C" & "D" Coys. will be stacked with the Company blankets. Mess Kits will be carried on the Field Kitchens.

6. **BILLETING.** Arrangements will be notified later.

7. **SICK PARADE.** Sick Parade will be held at 08.15 hours.

8. **ACKNOWLEDGE.**

(Signed) L.W. Shepherdson.
Captain, A/Adjutant,
20th Bn. DURHAM LIGHT INFANTRY.

13-12-1918.

Copy No. 1   Filed.
Copy No. 2. O.C. "A" Coy.
Copy No. 3. O.C. "B" Coy.
Copy No. 4. O.C. "C" Coy.
Copy No. 5. O.C. "D" Coy.
Copy No. 6. Quartermaster. O.C.H.Q.
Copy No. 7. Transport-Officer. Quartermaster.
Copy No. 8. Transport Officer.
Copy No. 9. Medical Officer.
Copy No. 10. R.S.M.
Copy No. 11. War Diary.

APP IV

SECRET.   20TH BN. DURHAM LIGHT INFANTRY.   COPY NO......
                    ORDER NO.196.

            Reference Map - BRUSSELS 1/100,000.

1. **INTENTION.** The Battalion will continue the march tomorrow, the 16th December 1918 and proceed to the GENAPPE area.

2. **INSTRUCTIONS.** "B" & "A" Companies and Transport will parade at 09.15 hours on the 2nd class road leading to their billets, with the head of the column at the junction of that road with the main road.
   "D" & "C" Companies and H.Q. will parade on the main road at 09.15 hours with the head of the column at the junction of the main road with the 2nd class road leading to A & B Coys' billets.

   ORDER OF MARCH.   "D","C",H.Q.,"B" & "A" Companies, Transport.

   DISTANCES.   The usual distances will be maintained on the march.

3. **TRANSPORT.**   The Medical Cart will report to the R.A.P. and the Mess Cart to H.Q. Mess at 09.15 hours.

4. **BLANKETS.**   Blankets will be stacked outside Coy. H.Qrs at 08.00 hours.

5. **OFFICERS' VALISES & MESS KITS.** The Officers' valises of "A","B" & Headquarters will be stacked outside their respective H.Qrs by 08.00 hours, for collection by Transport.
   The Officers' valises of "C" & "D" Companies will be stacked with the blankets by the same hour for collection by lorry.
   Officers' Mess Kits will be carried on Field Kitchens.

6. **SICK PARADE.**   07.00 hours.

7. **ACKNOWLEDGE.**

                        (SGD) L.W. SHEPHERDSON,
                              Capt. A/Adjutant,
15-12-18.   20th Bn. Durham Light Infantry.

Copy No. 1.   Filed.
Copy No. 2.   O.C. "A" Company.
Copy No. 3.   O.C. "B" Company.
Copy No. 4.   O.C. "C" Company.
Copy No. 5.   O.C. "D" Company.
Copy No. 6.   O.C. Headquarters.
Copy No. 7.   Quartermaster.
Copy No. 8.   Transport Officer.
Copy No. 9.   Medical Officer.
Copy No. 10. R.S.M.
Copy No. 11. War Diary.

APP V

SECRET.   20TH BN. DURHAM LIGHT INFANTRY.   Copy No,,
                ORDER NO. 107.

            Reference Map - BRUSSELS 1/100,000.

1. INTENTION.   The Battalion will continue the march tomorrow,
17th inst. and will proceed to the LIGNY Area.

2. INSTRUCTIONS. The Battalion will form up ni column of route
on the GENAPPE - QUATRE BRAS Road with the Head of the Column
at the Railway Crossing GENAPPE and ready to move off at 09.15 hours.

DRESS. - Full Marching Order.

ORDER OF MARCH.- "A","B","C" & "D" Companies, H.Q. & TRansport.

DISTANCES. The usual distances will be maintained on the march.

ROUTE.- QUATRE BRAS - SOMBREFFE Road.

3. TRANSPORT.   The Medical Cart will report to the R.A.P. and the
Mess Cart to H.Q. Mess at 08.00 hours.

4. BLANKETS.   Blankets will be stacked outside Coy.H.Qrs at
08.00 hours.

5. OFFICERS' VALISES & MESS KITS. The Officers' valises of "A","B",
and H.Q. will be stacked outside their respective Headquarters
by 08.00 hours for collection by Transport.
                    The Officers' valises of "C" & "D"
Companies will be stacked outside their respective H.Qrs with the
Blankets by the same hour for collection by lorry.
                    Officers, Mess Kits will be carried
on Field Kitchens.

6. SICK PARADE.   07.00 hours.

7. BILLETING.   Instructions will be notified later.

8. ACKNOWLEDGE.

                        (Sgd) L.W. SHEPHERDSON,
                            Capt. A/Adjutant,
16-12-18.   20th Bn. Durham Light Infantry.

Copy No. 1.   Filed.
Copy No. 2.   O.C. "A" Company.
Copy No. 3.   O.C. "B" Company.
Copy No. 4.   O.C. "C" Company.
Copy No. 5.   O.C. "D" Company.
Copy No. 6.   Quartermaster.
Copy No. 7.   Transport Officer.
Copy No. 8.   O.C. H.Q.
Copy No. 9.   Medical Officer.

APP. VI

SECRET.   20TH BN. DURHAM LIGHT INFANTRY.   Copy No.....
           ORDER NO. 108.

Ref.Maps - BRUSSELS & NAMUR.

1. INTENTION.   The Battalion will continue the march tomorrow, the 18th inst. and will proceed to the TEMPLOUX Area.

2. INSTRUCTIONS.   The Battalion will parade in column of route on the LIGNE - BOIGNE Road with the head of the Column at the Railway Station immediately S.W. of the L.in LIGNY, and ready to move off at 08.30 hours.

DRESS - Full Marching Order.

ORDER OF MARCH. H.Q., "B", "C", "D" & "A" Companies, Transport.

DISTANCES - The usual distances will be maintained on the march.

ROUTE - S.P., - BOIGNEE - ST. MARTIN - Cross Roads 1 Kilo. S.W. of ONOZ - ONOZ - SPY Station - SPY.

3. TRANSPORT.   The Medical Cart will report to the R.A.P. and the Mess Cart to H.Q. Mess at 07.30 hours.

4. BLANKETS.   Blankets will be stacked outside Company Headquarters by 07.30 hours.

5. OFFICERS' VALISES & MESS KITS. The Officers' valises of H.Q., "A" & "B" Companies will be stacked outside their respective Company Headquarters by 07.30 hours for collection by Transport.

    The officers' valises of "C" & "D" Companies will be stacked with the Company Blankets by the same hour for collection by lorry.

6. SICK PARADE - 06.30 hours.

7. BILLETING.   Instructions will be issued as early as possible.

8. ACKNOWLEDGE.

                    (sgd) L.W. SHEPHERDSON,
                             Capt. A/Adjutant,
17-12-18.   20th Bn. Durham Light Infantry.

Copy No. 1. Filed.
Copy No. 2. O.C. "A" Company.
Copy No. 3. O.C. "B" Company.
Copy No. 4. O.C. "C" Company.
Copy No. 5. O.C. "D" Company.
Copy No. 6. O.C. H.Q.
Copy No. 7. Quartermaster.
Copy No. 8. Transport Officer.
Copy No. 9. Medical Officer.
Copy No. 10. R.S.M.
Copy No. 11. War Diary.

LONDON DIVISION
(LATE 41ST DIVISION)
124TH INFY BDE

20TH BN DURHAM LT INFY
JAN - FEB 1919

Northern Div 7.

Jan–Feb 1919.

Army Form C. 2118.

20th Battalion
Durham Light Infantry

WAR DIARY
or
INTELLIGENCE SUMMARY.
(Erase heading not required.)

Place	Date 1919 JAN.	Hour	Summary of Events and Information	Remarks and references to Appendices
BILLETS ANTHEIT	1		Weather – dry. New Year's Day was observed as a holiday. DIVINE SERVICE was held in the LECTURE ROOM of the SCHOOL.	
– do –	2		Weather – showery. In the forenoon the EDUCATIONAL CLASSES continued and recreational training was carried out in the afternoon.	
– do –	3		Weather – wet. In the morning Companies when not engaged in Educational Work were at the disposal of Coy Commdr. Recreational training was carried out in the afternoon. In the evening a lecture by the Commanding Officer on "AUSTRALIA" was given in the SCHOOL.	
– do –	4		Weather – wet. Educational Classes continued in the morning and recreational training was carried out in the afternoon.	
– do –	5		Weather – dull. DIVINE SERVICE was held in the morning in the SCHOOL.	
– do –	6		Weather – dull. The battalion proceeded by March Route to HUY NORD STA. HUY and entrained for the COLOGNE bridgehead. The train moved off at 1800 hrs. and travelled via LIÈGE and VERVIERS.	App 1

Army Form C. 2118.

WAR DIARY
or
INTELLIGENCE SUMMARY.
(Erase heading not required.)

Instructions regarding War Diaries and Intelligence Summaries are contained in F.S. Regs., Part II. and the Staff Manual respectively. Title pages will be prepared in manuscript.

Place	Date	Hour	Summary of Events and Information	Remarks and references to Appendices
BILLETS — ENGELS-KIRCHEN.	1919 JAN. 7		Weather- fine. The battalion crossed into GERMANY at HERBESTHAL at 0015 hr. on the train, and was carried via AIX-LA-CHAPELLE and COLOGNE to HOFFNUNGSTHAL where it detrained at 10.30 hrs. In the afternoon it proceeded by ROUTE MARCH to ENGELSKIRCHEN and took over an OUTPOST LINE from 48TH CANADIAN REGT. of HIGHLANDERS.	J.L.
- do -	8		Weather- fine. In the morning battalion was on OUTPOST DUTY. In the afternoon those not on duty were engaged in recreational training.	J.L.
- do -	9		Weather- fine. Battalion on outpost duty. School at ENGELSKIRCHEN (2 rooms) taken over for EDUCATIONAL purposes. Afternoon - recreational training.	J.L.
- do -	10		Weather- fine. Battalion on outpost duty. Recreational training in afternoon.	J.L.
- do -	11		Weather- fine. Battalion on outpost duty. KIT inspection in morning. Recreational training in the afternoon.	J.L.
- do -	12		Weather- wet. Battalion on outpost duty. DIVINE SERVICE was held in the school ENGELSKIRCHEN.	J.L.

Army Form C. 2118.

WAR DIARY
or
INTELLIGENCE SUMMARY.
(Erase heading not required.)

Instructions regarding War Diaries and Intelligence Summaries are contained in F. S. Regs., Part II. and the Staff Manual respectively. Title pages will be prepared in manuscript.

Place	Date 1919	Hour	Summary of Events and Information	Remarks and references to Appendices
OUTPOSTS ENGELS - KIRCHEN	JAN 13		Weather - wet. Battalion on outpost duty. In the morning EDUCATIONAL CLASSES were re-opened, and Companies carried out drill. In the afternoon, recreational training was carried out.	J.6.
-do-	14		Weather - wet. Battalion on OUTPOST DUTY. In the morning the EDUCATIONAL CLASSES were re-opened, and those not otherwise engaged, carried out drill. In the afternoon, recreational training was carried on.	J.6.
-do-	15		Wet. Battalion on Outpost Duty. In the morning close order drill was carried out by Companies. The afternoon was devoted to Recreational Training.	J.6.
-do-	16		Weather - wet. Battalion on Outpost Duty. In the morning EDUCATIONAL CLASSES were held and CLOSE ORDER DRILL was carried out. Recreational training in afternoon.	J.6.
-do-	17		Weather - dull. Batt. on OUTPOST DUTY. In the morning EDUCATIONAL CLASSES were held + drill carried out. In the afternoon, recreational training took place.	J.6.
-do-	18		Weather - slight fall of snow. Batt. on Outpost duty. In the morning COYS. carried out Interior Economy work. Recreational training in afternoon.	J.6.
-do-	19		Weather fine. Batt. on Outpost duty. DIVINE SERVICE in morning in the School. In the afternoon "D" Coy. played agst. 187 Batt. R.F.A. (DIV. TOURNAMENT) drawn by 1goal to nil.	J.6.

(A9175) Wt W235/P360 600,000 12/17 D.D.&L. Sch. 53a. Forms/C2118/15.

Army Form C. 2118.

WAR DIARY
or
INTELLIGENCE SUMMARY.
(Erase heading not required.)

Instructions regarding War Diaries and Intelligence Summaries are contained in F. S. Regs., Part II. and the Staff Manual respectively. Title pages will be prepared in manuscript.

Place	Date 1919	Hour	Summary of Events and Information	Remarks and references to Appendices
OUTPOSTS ENGELS- KIRCHEN.	JAN. 20		Weather-fine. In the morning those not engaged in OUTPOST DUTY of EDUCATIONAL WORK carried out DRILL. In the afternoon, recreational training was arranged.	J.B.
- do -	21		Weather-fine. Battⁿ on Outpost Duty. Classes + Drill were carried on in the morning, and in the afternoon recreational training took place.	J.B.
- do -	22		Weather - fine but cold. Battⁿ on Outpost Duty. In the morning EDUCATIONAL CLASSES were held and close order drill carried out. In the afternoon recreational training was indulged in.	J.B.
- do -	23		Weather - fine and cold. Battⁿ on Outpost Duty. In the morning close order drill was carried out. recreational training took place in the afternoon.	J.B.
- do -	24		Weather - fine and cold. Battⁿ on Outpost Duty. In the morning EDUCATIONAL CLASSES were held and drill carried out. In the afternoon recreational training took place.	J.B.
- do -	25		Weather - dull. Battⁿ on Outpost Duty. In the morning Steam Tranny Parade was held. Recreational Training was carried out in the afternoon.	J.B.
- do -	26		Weather - cold. DIVINE SERVICE was held in the morning and the SCHOOL ENGELSKIRCHEN. The battalion was on Outpost Duty.	J.B.

WAR DIARY
or
INTELLIGENCE SUMMARY.
(Erase heading not required.)

Army Form C. 2118.

Place	Date	Hour	Summary of Events and Information	Remarks and references to Appendices
OUTPOSTS	1919 JAN.			
ENGELSKIRCHEN	27		Weather – Snowy. Battⁿ on Outpost Duty. In the morning SCHOOL was held and company drill carried out. The afternoon was devoted to recreational training	/6.
–do–	28		Weather – Snowy. Battⁿ on Outpost Duty. In the morning SCHOOL was held and drill carried out. A considerable number of men were sent home for demobilisation. In the afternoon recreational training was indulged in.	/6.
–do–	29		Weather – Snowy. Battⁿ on Outpost Duty. In the morning Companies carried out Arms and Squad Drill. The afternoon was given up to recreational training.	/6.
–do–	30		Weather – Snowy. Battⁿ on Outpost Duty. In the morning SCHOOL was held and drill carried out. The afternoon was devoted to skating and other forms of recreational training.	/6.
–do–	31		Weather – Cold. Battⁿ on Outpost Duty. SCHOOL was held in the morning and recreational training in the afternoon.	/6.

Wm Vaughn. Lt Col.
Comm^{dg}. 20/Bⁿ Durham L.I.

SECRET.   20TH BN. DURHAM LIGHT INFANTRY.   Copy No......

ORDER NO. 111.

Reference Map - LIEGE Sheet 7 1/100,000.

1. **INTENTION.** The Battalion will proceed by march route to HUY (Nord) Station to entrain for the COLOGNE area. On arrival in the latter area, the Battalion will relieve the 1st Canadian Division in the ENGELSKIRCHEN area.

2. **INSTRUCTIONS.**

(a) <u>Starting Point</u> - Cross Roads immediately West of E in LA HERBATE
(b) <u>Time of Passing S.P.</u> - 12.40 hours.
(c) <u>Order of March</u> - H.Q., D, B, A & C Companies.
(d) <u>Distances</u> - The usual distances will be maintained on the march.
(e) <u>Transport</u> - The Transport will proceed to the station independently, the Head of the column to pass S.P. at 12.30 hours. The Maltese Cart will report to the Aid Post at 08.00 hours.
(f) <u>Halts</u> - The Battalion will halt from 12.30 to 13.00 hours.
(g) <u>Officers' Kits</u> - Officers' Valises will be stacked at Company H.Qrs. by 08.30 hours. Officers will make their own arrangements for Mess Kits required on the train to be carried to the station. Mess Kits NOT required on the train will be carried on Field Kitchens.
The Transport Officer will arrange for the collection of Valises.
The Mess Cart will report at H.Q. Mess at 09.15 hours.
(h) <u>Blankets</u> - Blankets, rolled in bundles of 10 and labelled, will be stacked at Coy.H.Qrs by 08.15 hours, for collection by lorry. O's.C.Companies will send guides for the lorries to report at Orderly Room at 08.30 hours tomorrow.
(i) <u>Stove Boilers & Camp Kettles</u> - These will be carried on Lewis Gun Limbers. L.G. Limbers will report to Companies at 09.00 hours and will be loaded immediately.
(k) <u>Rations</u> - The unconsumed portion of tomorrow's rations and rations for the 7th inst. will be carried on the man.
(l) <u>Sanitation</u> - O's.C. Coys, O.C. H.Qrs. & Transport Officer will ensure that billets are left scrupulously clean and that all latrines are properly filled in. A certificate that this order has been complied with will be handed to the Adjutant at the station.
(m) <u>Area Stores</u> - All latrine buckets and stoves will be returned to the R.E. Stores by 08.30 hours, tomorrow.
(n) <u>Unloading Party</u> - O.C. "D" Company will detail a party of 2 Officers and 50 O.R. for detraining party on arrival at detraining station.
(o) <u>Detraining Station</u> - Possible detraining station HOFFNUNGSTHAL, COLOGNE - MUHLHEIM or MESCHEID.
(p) <u>Relief</u> - Details for relief of a Bn. of the 1st Canadian Division will be notified later.

3. **ACKNOWLEDGE.**

(signature)
Captain A/Adjutant,
20th Bn. Durham Light Infantry.

6-1-1919.

Issued to all recipients of Warning Order No 1 at 19.10 hours.

3. 41st Divisional War Standing Orders
2. Trench Standing Orders, 124° Inf. Bde
2. Staff Manual 1912
5. Field Service Regulations Part 1. Operations
2. "   "   "   Part 2. Organisation & Administration
1. Musketry Regulations Part. 1
1. Field Artillery Training 1914.
1. Notes on Coy & Platoon Drill 1916
1. Methods of Unarmed Attack & Defence (1917)
1. Supplementary Physical Training Tables (1916)
1. Suggested syllabus of course for Army Musketry Camps.
1. Notes for ADCs of Batteries & Coy Commanders on Trench Routine 41st Divn
1. Fourth Army Training arrangements
8. Hints on Training
1. Manual of Map reading & Field Sketching (1912)
2. Handbook for .303 in. Lewis Gun (Oct 1918)

1.	S.S. 112	Consolidation of trenches localities & craters after assault & capture with a note on rapid wiring. (1916)
1	S.S. 116	Notes on cover against shell fire (July 1916)
1	S.S. 122	Notes on Lewis & Machine Guns (Sept. 1916)
✓1	S.S. 123	Notes on use of carrier pigeons in France.
1	S.S. 130	Notes on employment of 4" Stokes Mortar Bombs.
1	S.S. 131	Co-operation of aircraft with Artillery.
1	S.S. 135	Training and employment of Divisions 1918 (Jan 1918)
1	"	Instructions for training of Divisions for Offensive Action (Dec 1916)
1	"	Division in Attack
6	S.S. 137	Recreational Training
1	S.S. 139/3	Artillery Notes. Counter Battery work
1	S.S. 141	Communication by Wireless (March 1918)
2	S.S. 142	Provisional notes on firing at Aircraft with Machine Guns & other small Arms.
1	S.S. 143	Training & employment of Platoons 1918.
1	S.S. 145	Notes on Engineer work during operation (Jan. 1918)
1	S.S. 152	Instructions for training British Armies in France (Jan. 1918)
4	S.S. 153	Notes on the '08 (Heavy) and '08/15 (Light German Machine Guns

List of Pamphlets & Books

1.	S.S. 167	Signal organization for heavy Branch, Machine Gun Corps. (August 1917)
1.	S.S. 168	Notes on employment of serviceable guns and Trench Mortars captured from the enemy. (June 1917)
✓2.	S.S. 169	Employment of 3" Stokes Mortars in Recent Fighting (June 1917)
1.	S.S. 170	Notes on Co-operation between aircraft and artillery during recent operations on 2nd Army front (June 1917)
1.	S.S. 172	Preliminary Notes on Recent Operations on Front of Second Army. (July 1917)
2.	S.S. 173	Notes on Screens. (July 1917).
2.	S.S. 177	Instructions on Wiring (Aug. 1917)
1	S.S. 182	Instructions on Bombing Part. I (Dec. 1917)
✓2	S.S. 183	Light (Stokes) Mortar Drill (Sept 1917)
2	S.S. 185.	Assault Training (Sept 1917)
1	S.S. 187	Attack on LAFFAUX (Oct. 1917)
1	S.S. 188	Offence versus Defence in the air (Oct. 1917)
1	S.S. 189	Light Mortar Training
2	S.S. 190	Rifle Grenade Discharger No 1 Mark 1 (Oct. 1917)
2	S.S. 191	Intercommunication in the Field. (Nov. 1917)
2	S.S. 192	Employment of Machine Guns part I July 1918
1	S.S. 192	ditto Part II

3

1	S.S. 193	Standing Orders for Defence against Gas. (Oct. 1917)
2	S.S. 196	Diagram of Field Defences (March 1918)
3	S.S. 197	Tactical Employment of Lewis Guns
	S.S. 201/3/a	Machine Gun Notes (1918)
1	S.S. 202	Organization of Shell hole Defences. (Dec. 1917)
2	S.S. 206	Principles and Practice of Camouflage. (March 1918)
2	S.S. 210	Division in Defence. (May 1918)
1	S.S. 204	Carrier Pigeons in war (March 1918)
1	S.S. 212	Yellow Cross Gas Shells and the Measures to be taken to counteract their effects
1	S.S. 390	Special publications
3	S.S. 408	Questions a Platoon Commander should ask himself on taking over a trench and at Intervals afterwards
1	S.S. 415	Duties of an Officer. Knowledge & Character
1	S.S. 534	Defence against gas. (March 1918)
1	S.S. 541	Ration Pamphlet
5	S.S. 724	March discipline and Traffic Control

LIST OF FILES.

1. Operation Orders.   (1) Brigade.
                        (2) Divn.
                        (3) Other Sources.

2. Courses of Instruction.

3. Defence Schemes.   Correspondence re.
                                    Defences.

4. Brigade Conferences.

5. Miscellaneous.

6. Correspondence re. Machine Guns & Trench Mortars.

7. Telephones & Signals. Codes. etc.

8. Lectures and Demonstrations.

9. (1) Intelligence Summaries.
   (2)   "   General.

10. Training (ordinary).

11. Recreational Training.
    (1) General Correspondence.
    (2) Football.
    (3) Cross Country Runs.
    (4) Boxing.
    (5) Training. Kit.

12. General Correspondence re. Outposts Line etc.

WAR DIARY
INTELLIGENCE SUMMARY

(Erase heading not required.)

Army Form C. 2118

Instructions regarding War Diaries and Intelligence Summaries are contained in F. S. Regs., Part II. and the Staff Manual respectively. Title pages will be prepared in manuscript.

20 D 1 / 34

Place	Date 1919 FEB.	Hour	Summary of Events and Information	Remarks and references to Appendices
OUTPOSTS ENGELSKIRCHEN	1		Weather – cold. Battn. on outpost duty. In the morning drill was carried out. In the afternoon "D" Coy. played against the 23rd Battn. MIDDLESEX REGT. in the Semi-Final of the DIVISIONAL FOOTBALL TOURNAMENT and won by 2 goals to 1.	
– do –	2		Weather – cold. Battn. on outpost duty. In the morning DIVINE SERVICE was held.	
– do –	3		Weather – cold and frosty. Battn. on Outpost Duty. A rehearsal of the ceremonial drill required for the PRESENTATION of the colours took place.	
– do –	4		Weather – cold. Battn. on outpost duty. In the morning the Divisional Commdt. witnessed a rehearsal of the PRESENTATION of the colours parade. Recreational training in afternoon.	
– do –	5		Weather – cold and frosty. Battn. on Outpost Duty. In the morning school was held. Recreational training took place in the afternoon.	
– do –	6		Weather very cold. Battn. on Outpost Duty. In the morning the battalion carried out arms drill. The final match of the DIVISIONAL Inter Coy. FOOTBALL TOURNAMENT was played in the afternoon between "D Coy. Somus and D.A.C. "D" Coy won by 1 goal to nil.	
– do –	7		Weather – cold. Battn. on Outpost Duty. In the morning a lecture on "FRANCE & FRENCH PEOPLE" was given. Recreational training was carried out in the afternoon.	
– do –	8		Weather very cold. Battn. on Outpost Duty. Drill in morning. Recreational training afternoon.	

Army Form C. 2118.

WAR DIARY
or
INTELLIGENCE SUMMARY.
(Erase heading not required.)

Instructions regarding War Diaries and Intelligence Summaries are contained in F. S. Regs., Part II. and the Staff Manual respectively. Title pages will be prepared in manuscript.

Place	Date 1919	Hour	Summary of Events and Information	Remarks and references to Appendices
OUTPOSTS ENGELSKIRCHEN	FEB 9		Weather - very cold. Batt: on Outpost Duty. Divine Service was held in the morning	Ye.
- do -	10		Weather - cold & frosty. Batt: on Outpost Duty. The UNION FLAG was presented to	
EHRESHOVEN	11		the battalion at EHRESHOVEN by the 2nd ARMY COMMANDER, GENERAL SIR H. PLUMER	Ye.
			Weather - cold & frosty - Battalion were relieved on outpost system by the 10th Battn.	
			"Queen's" R.W. Surrey Regiment and moved to Billets in support area with 2 coys	Yes.
			situated at LOOPE + 1 at VILKERATH, B.HQ being established at EHRESHOVEN	
- do -	12		Weather - cold & frosty - boy's carried out drill inspections during the morning -	Yes.
			Afternoon was devoted to recreational training	
- do -	13		Weather - mild - boys carried out drill & inspections during the morning - Afternoon	Yes.
			was devoted to recreational training - Capt. W. Johnson left battalion on being	
			demobilised.	
- do -	14		Weather - mild - boys carried out drill & inspections during the morning - Ye. -	Yes.
			Commanding Officer inspected "A" company in full marching order - Afternoon	
			was devoted to recreational training	
- do -	15		Weather - mild - During the morning coys carried out interior economy - "B" coy	Yes.
			was inspected by the Commanding Officer - Afternoon was devoted to recreational	
			training. Cross country race and inter coy team	

Army Form C. 2118.

WAR DIARY
or
INTELLIGENCE SUMMARY.
(Erase heading not required.)

Instructions regarding War Diaries and Intelligence Summaries are contained in F. S. Regs., Part II. and the Staff Manual respectively. Title pages will be prepared in manuscript.

Place	Date	Hour	Summary of Events and Information	Remarks and references to Appendices
BILLETS. EHRESHOVEN	FEB. 16		Weather - rainy during morning & night - Divine Services were held during the morning - Afternoon - Battalion football team played 10th Battn. "Queens" R.W. Surrey Regt in the Army Competition and won by 4 goals to 3	Hqrs.
-do-	17		Weather - showery - "A" & "B" Coys carried out training during the morning. The Commanding Officer inspected C & D Coys + Headquarters - The afternoon was devoted to Recreational Training	Hqrs.
-do-	18.		Weather showery - Coys carried out training in the morning - Afternoon - recreational training	Hqrs.
-do-	19.		Weather fine - "A" company devoted the day to training in the use of weapons - tactics - "C" company acted as duty Coy for the day - B & D Coys carried out training inspections - Afternoon recreational training	Hqrs.
-do-	20.		Weather rainy - bonfires carried out training during morning - Afternoon devoted to Recreational training.	Hqrs.
-do-	21		Weather showery - bonfires carried out training during morning - Coy Commanders reconnoitred line of resistance - Afternoon recreational training	Hqrs.

Army Form C. 2118.

WAR DIARY
INTELLIGENCE SUMMARY.
(Erase heading not required.)

Instructions regarding War Diaries and Intelligence Summaries are contained in F.S. Regs., Part II. and the Staff Manual respectively. Title pages will be prepared in manuscript.

Place	Date 1919	Hour	Summary of Events and Information	Remarks and references to Appendices
BILLETS. EHRESHOVEN	Feby. 22		Weather showery – boys carried out interior economy during the morning – Afternoon – devoted to recreational training, the Battalion football team played 26th Battn. Royal Fusiliers in Army competition – Result draw 1 goal each.	Ans.
– do –	23		Weather fine but dull – Divine Services were held during morning.	Ans.
– do –	24		Weather showery – Companies carried out training during morning – Afternoon – Recreational training – Battalion football team played 26th Battn. Royal Fusiliers in Army competition – Result draw 1 goal each.	Ans.
– do –	25		Weather showery – Bde. & Divl. Commanders French inspections were postponed on account of weather – companies carried out training – lectures in billets – Afternoon recreational training – A boy ½ hype B coy at football result Bcoy 1 goal A coy nil	Ans.
– do –	26		Weather fine – Bde. & Divl. commander inspected the Battn. during the morning – Afternoon – Recreational training – Advance parties proceeded to Cologne to take over billets of (82nd Bde) 150 3rd Battn. Grenadier Guards – commanding officer & left Battalion on being demobilised	Ans.

Army Form C. 2118.

WAR DIARY
INTELLIGENCE SUMMARY.
(Erase heading not required.)

Place	Date	Hour	Summary of Events and Information	Remarks and references to Appendices
BILLETS. EHRESHOVEN	1919 FEB. 27.		Weather fine during morning - showery during afternoon. - Battn. proceeded by march route to OVERATH station and entrained at 4 p.m. Transport horses were handed over to 1/4th Middlesex Regt. - Battalion detrained at NIPPES station at 8 p.m. proceeded to RIEHL BARRACKS occupied billets vacated by 3rd Battn. GRENADIER GUARDS.	the the
BARRACKS RIEHL	28.		Weather fine - boys carried out training in ceremonial & guards during morning - Afternoon recreational training	the the

Cannell Major
Commdg 20th Bn Durham L.I.

www.ingramcontent.com/pod-product-compliance
Lightning Source LLC
Chambersburg PA
CBHW081544160426
43191CB00011B/1833